DENIED
3
TIMES

By

Will Clark

Denied
3
Times

Copyright © 2014 by Will Clark

ISBN 13: 978-1500351724
10: 1500351725

Published by
Motivation Basics
P.O. Box 6327
Diamondhead, MS 39525
Will01@aol.com

QUOTE

"A nation can survive its fools, and even the ambitious. But it cannot survive treason from within. An enemy at the gates is less formidable, for he is known and carries his banner openly. But the traitor moves amongst those within the gate freely, his sly whispers rustling through all the alleys, heard in the very halls of government itself. For the traitor appears not a traitor; he speaks in accents familiar to his victims, and he wears their face and their arguments, he appeals to the baseness that lies deep in the hearts of all men. He rots the soul of a nation, he works secretly and unknown in the night to undermine the pillars of the city, he infects the body politic so that it can no longer resist. A murderer is less to fear. The traitor is the plague." *Marcus Tullius Cicero, 58 B.C. Speech in the Roman Senate*

CONTENTS

Introduction   7

Chapter 1   Barack Hussein Obama   11

Chapter 2   The War Against Christians   21

Chapter 3   More War Against Christians   39

Chapter 4   America's Most Biblically-Hostile
             President   55

Chapter 5   Why the Hatred for Christianity   79

Chapter 6   Related Articles   101

Conclusion   119

About the Author   123

Things We Must Never Forget   125

Greatest Quotes of our Time   127

Other Books by the Author   129

Introduction

At the Lord's Supper, Jesus told Peter that he would deny Jesus three times before the rooster crowed. Jesus was arrested that night, and as he had said, Peter denied knowing Jesus three times before the rooster crowed. Jesus looked Peter in the eyes as the rooster crowed. Peter wept in an action titled, The Repentance of Peter.

Isn't it ironic and prophetic that God's name was denied three times at the 2012 Democratic National Convention? Not once, not twice, but three times the convention members, by voice vote, chose not to include God's name in the party platform. After the third vote, the chairman falsely claimed the vote had been two-thirds in the affirmative, and God's name and the recognition of Jerusalem were put back in the platform.

Was the prophesy by Jesus regarding Peter a hidden message about how God would be rejected at a later time? Was Peter used as an example to warn of humankind's modern-day denial of God? Why was God's name removed from the platform in the first place? What pressure, and from whom was someone forced to take that action? Only one man had enough power and authority to force that omission. Obama got caught, and his blasphemy against

God was exposed. That blasphemy continued on the convention floor and was tolerated by his followers. That prophetic rooster crowed over 2000 years ago.

How many of his followers outside the convention are influenced by this Pied Piper also to reject God? Peter showed his repentance. Has there been any repentance from any of Obama's followers on the convention floor, or elsewhere?

Who is this man, Barack Hussein Obama? Does anyone really know? What are his secrets and deceptions? Is he the one destined to lead the world on its path to moral destruction? Before that happens will we be warned again by a rooster crowing three times - or by many other signs?

This is the link to that latest three denials at the Democratic Convention. No roosters were crowing, but many in the audience were protesting when the chairman falsely claimed there were enough affirmative votes to put the reference to God and Jerusalem back in the Democratic platform:

http://www.youtube.com/watch?v=fAwlyYyiIS4

Who is this man, Barack Hussein Obama, who claims to be a Christian but offers no indication he worships the true God? Within most of his actions and rhetoric he seems to worship no one other than himself, although he is very familiar with the Koran and in an earlier time was very precise at reciting passages from that source. That recitation and other comments regarding religion and worship strongly suggest he has a basis or a foundation in the Islamic faith. Who is this man who considers himself a leader and has such influence that makes people turn from God and the

Christian foundations that made our country, the United States of America, great.

Nearly all Americans in our past worshiped God to give thanks for the creation of our country and for its great blessings. Through Obama's leadership and influence God's name now has been cast out and unwelcome from many institutions in America. How far will these exclusions go; perhaps to the point of total exclusions and even persecution? Does not evil and persecution left unchecked become more acceptable and normal; does it not often lead to tyranny? How can evil be recognized and judged in a society not influenced by the respect for God's creation? Will Obama's influence create a condition that one day will cause Christians and Jews to flee to the wilderness? Perhaps this war on Christians is foretold in Revelations, Chapter 12. Pertinent verses in the chapter include:

"And there appeared a great wonder in heaven; a woman clothed with the sun, and the moon under her feet, and upon her head a crown of twelve stars." (Have you ever heard of the twelve tribes of Israel?)

Verse 2: "And she being with child cried, travailing in birth, and pained to be delivered." (Wasn't there much persecution of believers in the beginning of Christianity?)

Verse 4: "----- and the dragon stood before the woman which was ready to be delivered, for to devour her child as soon as it was born."(The Devil is always lurking to destroy those who believe in Jesus.)

Verse 5: "And she brought forth a man child, who was to rule all nations with a rod of iron; and her child was caught up unto God, and to his throne."

Verse 6: and the woman fled into the wilderness, where she hath a place prepared of God, that they should feed her there for a thousand two hundred and threescore days." (The abomination of desolation - when the place of God in Jerusalem will be occupied by the beast and his forces. Jews are warned to flee. Many believe this place of God will be the rebuilt temple.)

Verse 17: "And the dragon was wroth with the woman, and went to make war with the remnant of her seed, which keep the commandments of God, and have the testimony of Jesus Christ."(Does this not describe the present day war on Christianity: the mention of God and Jesus in many public places?)

Although John wrote Revelation, the Apocalypse, two thousand years ago while exiled on the Island of Patmos by Emperor Domitian, many of his written visions seem more relevant today than in the past. History, events, and communications seem destined to explain his visions more every day. One merely has to look, read, and listen with an open and objective spirit. Judeo-Christians are now being persecuted and belittled throughout the world; even beheaded in many places. How soon until they flee to the wilderness? Let's begin to understand that answer by examining the one now considered the leader of the free world and his influence on forces that might allow and encourage those dangers to Judeo-Christian followers - Barack Hussein Obama.

Chapter 1

Barack Hussein Obama

Is He Knowledgeable?

Is Barack Obama a patriotic man, a loyal man, an honest man, a religious man, a knowledgeable man, a man concerned only about America's future. To whom does he pray; to whom is he patriotic; and what are his plans for America's future?

Is he as knowledgeable and astute as he pretends? Is he really an American citizen? Many people think not. Wouldn't an American citizen know America is comprised of fifty states. Early on, Obama made reference to the fifty-seven states. According to him there are fifty-seven states in the United States. I can't find the other seven. Maybe my maps are outdated. Maybe I need new glasses. Even if he were in an environment during his youth outside the United States certainly he would have seen an American flag. All he had to do was to count the number of stars in the flag. On the other hand, did he have enough love and respect for the American flag to even look at it? He recites many passages of the Koran with accuracy and precision. One might ask which object commands more of his attention and respect.

Is He Honest?

An American, a real American, gives much consideration to those two personal traits. We expect our friends and associates to be honest with us and when they speak to others. Those are important traits and personal characteristics we define as making us human, especially in reference to Godliness, nature, and humanity. He has proven his lack of these important expectations of humanity, especially those of a leader, any leader.

His lies, falsehoods, and deceptions are too numerous to itemize in this short book. Two most recent and important ones include his words regarding the cause of the massacre in Benghazi, Libya. He knew that attack was simply from an Islamic terrorist attack, yet he boldly claimed it was caused by some Youtube video. And we can never forget his words regarding the Affordable Care Act (Obamacare.) "If you like your plan you can keep your plan. If you like your doctor, you can keep your doctor."

After he learned those promises were not true he continued to repeat them. In almost every important event where honesty might allow a weakness to his plans he has always chosen to be dishonest and deceptive. He is a deceiver. Is he one described in 2 John 1:7? "For many deceivers have gone out into the world, those who do not confess the coming of Jesus Christ in the flesh. Such a one is the deceiver and the antichrist."

Is He Loyal?

He is so loyal he said he would never kick his friend and mentor,

Jeremiah Wright, under the bus. Reverend Wright is still wiping unexplained tire marks off his face. If he can't be loyal to a friend, should he be expected to be loyal to anyone or anything - especially the foundation of a nation founded on the principles of Christianity?

He said he hardly knew his good friend and party pal, Bill Ayers, the man who expressed his patriotism with bombs against Americans. Ayers is also the man, along with his father, who helped launch Obama's political career. What loyalty principles does Obama support? Does accepting encouragement and help from one who expressed, and still expresses, disdain and hatred toward American principles demonstrate his loyalty to our country? What is his ultimate goal? Is it to encourage Americans and help make America an even better place for all its citizens? Where do his loyalties lie? And again, why does he remain untruthful and deceptive? Our nation, the United States, was founded on honesty, dedication, and trust in the Almighty.

Would one loyal and dedicated to one nation bow down to the leader of another nation? He said he did not bow down to the Saudi king, while photographs and video clearly show his act of bowing to the king.

He lied again, but his attempt to deceive was less important than the implication of the act itself. He bowed to the leader of the Muslim Brotherhood, the widespread group of organizations dedicated to the destruction of Western civilization, including the annihilation of the United States. Unless he had ties to that king or to his influence why would he honor that king with a bow - subservience?

Obama has used the words, "My Muslim faith," before. How, and in what connotation did he mean that statement? Did his subservient bow to that Muslim king, the leader of the Muslim Brotherhood, suggest a menacing possibility?

Is he Patriotic?

He voluntarily listened to Jeremiah Wright's anti-American rant for years in a church setting, yet claims he never heard any offensive or unpatriotic comments against America. Did Wright say, "God d*** America," just one time? Unlikely. Would anyone who shares American values remain in an audience of such anti-American rhetoric?

He said he would have only patriotic Americans in his administration. Whatever happened to his close socialist supporters and sidekicks, Van Jones and Anita Dunn? Maybe Anita left to visit her favorite philosopher, Mao Zedong. Van Jones is still out there, espousing patriotic socialism from the sidelines. Obama didn't disassociate himself from these two until they were exposed by outside pressure. I'm sure with his great patriotism guiding him, he will eliminate all the other socialists, communists, and others who wish America harm from his administration. I'm still waiting and waiting for the next one to be asked to resign. I'm still waiting.

Perhaps it will be a long wait. Obama and several of his close advisors were mentored in the 1970s by a card-carrying Communist named Frank Marshall Davis, who was also a friend of Obama's grandfather. Davis is also historically associated with at least two of Obama's other closest advisors - one being his personal advisor Valerie Jarret. Some believe Frank Marshall

Davis is Obama's real father. Comparisons of photographs certainly create that question. He looks nothing like the man who claimed to be his real father. Compare his photograph with that of Davis. You might be surprised. This is the link for that comparison:

http://search.aol.com/aol/image?q=frank+marshall+davis&v_t= customfirefoxright

Obama whispered to the Russian leader that he will have more flexibility to give them what they want during his next term. How did he know he would have a next term? What did the Russians want? If he needs more secret flexibility, what threat is there to the United States? Medvedev said he would pass the information along to Vladimir. Recently, Russia invaded and annexed the Crimea region with only little insignificant protest from Obama. Was that the deal he promised when he 'had more flexibility?'

Religion:

Reference: Bible, Book of Revelation, 13:5. "And there was given unto him a mouth speaking great things and blasphemies." 13:6. "And he opened his mouth in blasphemy against God, to blaspheme his name, and his tabernacle, and them that dwell in heaven." These references describe two characteristics of the 666 Beast in the Book of Revelation: oratory and blasphemy. In the book of Revelation the Antichrist is identified only as the Beast, not the Antichrist. How does Barack Obama fulfill this description? Did not Barack Obama rise to his high position through recognition of his great oratory - especially when he has a teleprompter?

He said he is not a Muslim, but during an interview with George

Stephanopoulos on September 7, 2008, he referenced, "My Muslim faith." If he is a Muslim, why does he continue to deny it? Revelation also identifies the 666 Beast as, 'The Deceiver.' When speaking of the Koran, he says, "The Holy Koran." When referencing the Bible, he says, "The Bible." Why does he consider the Koran holy and the Bible not holy?

On June 28, 2006, during his 'Call to Renewal' speech, he mocked three sections of the Bible, including the Sermon on the Mount, which he called 'so radical.' He asked, mockingly, "Can either of these be used to guide public policy?" This is part of his speech most often quoted, in parts:

"Moreover, given the increasing diversity of America's population, the dangers of sectarianism have never been greater. Whatever we once were, we are no longer just a Christian nation; we are also a Jewish nation, a Muslim nation, a Buddhist nation, a Hindu nation, and a nation of nonbelievers.

And even if we did have only Christians in our midst, if we expelled every non-Christian from the United States of America, whose Christianity would we teach in the schools? Would we go with James Dobson's, or Al Sharpton's? Which passages of Scripture should guide our public policy? Should we go with Leviticus, which suggests slavery is ok and that eating shellfish is abomination? How about Deuteronomy, which suggests stoning your child if he strays from the faith? Or should we just stick to the Sermon on the Mount - a passage that is so radical that it's doubtful that our own Defense Department would survive its application? So before we get carried away, let's read our bibles. Folks haven't been reading their bibles."

Those who listened to the spoken version of this speech heard him say, "We are no longer a Christian nation." Then he interjected the "not just" comment after that. What was his thinking during that correction? Was it a simple slip, or was he judging his audience to decide if the "not just" comment should be applied or deleted? His later war on Christian principles might suggest he really meant "We are no longer a Christian nation."

On April 16, 2009, he required the monogram for the name of Jesus be covered before he made his speech at Georgetown University. The monogram above an archway was covered with black painted plywood. Certainly he would not consider this blasphemy - black painted plywood covering the symbol of Jesus. This is a summary of that event reported by CNSNews.com:

"Amidst all of the American flags and presidential seals, there was something missing when President Barack Obama gave an economic speech at Georgetown University this week -- Jesus. The White House asked Georgetown to cover a monogram symbolizing Jesus' name in Gaston Hall, which Obama used for his speech, according to CNSNews.com. The gold "IHS" monogram inscribed on a pediment in the hall was covered over by a piece of black-painted plywood, and remained covered over the next day, CNSNews.com reported.

The Washington Times' Belief Blog asked the university about the presidential request: While the "IHS" directly behind where Obama spoke was covered over, CNSNews.com said the monogram was still visible in 26 other places in the hall during his speech. Those areas just weren't as prominent. The Belief Blog talked with the Rev. Thomas Reese, a senior fellow at the Woodstock Institute at Georgetown University, who said he didn't think "this is motivated by theology, but by communications strategy."

The blog also talked with Catholic University spokesman Victor Nakas, who felt a bit more strongly on the subject: "I can't imagine, as the bishops' university and the national university of the Catholic Church, that we would ever cover up our religious art or signage for any reason," Mr. Nakas wrote. "Our Catholic faith is integral to our identity as an institution of higher education."

Should this covering of the symbol of Jesus be considered another 'denial?' Perhaps Obama has set a new record. Peter denied Jesus only three times. Perhaps Obama and his close followers know no limit to the number of times they will deny Jesus and insult and disavow Christianity.

On September 29, 2009, at a gathering of the Gamaliel Organization, the members prayed to Barack Obama, "Deliver us, Obama." Revelation also reveals that the Antichrist will not be someone 'against' Christ, but who will pretend to be Christ, and try to take his place - or will be assumed to be Christ-like by his followers. He will be worshiped by his followers. This is the link to that prayer to Obama:

http://www.youtube.com/watch?v=L_3884G2s6A

Another video also sparked a lot of controversy as young Stephen actually appears to pray to Barack Obama rather than for him, closing his eyes tightly as he thanks Obama for all he's done:

"Barack Obama, thank you for doing everything and all the kind stuff. Thank you for all the stuff that you helped us with. Thank you for taking the courage and responsibility for everything you have done for us. And God has given you a special power and you are going to handle it just fine. You are good, Barack Obama and you are great and when you get older, you will be able to do great things. Love, Stephen. Barack Obama!"

Regina Young, the uploader of the video, titled it "Prayer for President Barack Obama," and captioned it, "The prayer that he wanted to say for our President is priceless," but others see it in a wholly different light.

Commenters have furiously weighed in, labeling the video blasphemous and criticizing the child's mother as well as Obama. Commenter TexasOpenCarry wrote, "Praying To Barack Obama? Wonder how the Lord God Almighty is taking that..." while newbirth35 said, "Idolatry. That sounds more like a prayer To Obama, not FOR him. How sad, and even sadder that you are proud of the poor kid doing this."

A Christian Post article drew comparisons between Young's video and others which raised Obama to a high pedestal, namely a so-called "student militant-style Obama youth group" video which cited him as an inspiration for later success, as well as a video of elementary school-age children singing a song about Obama's achievements. The Post wrote, "Both videos caused controversy for suggesting that African Americans view Obama as a higher being than a human." This is the link to that video:

http://www.youtube.com/watch?v=24jPh49B8NI

The list of Obama's anti-Christian actions, rhetoric, and blasphemies is too long to identify each individually. A casual review of his actions and comments against churches, especially the Catholic Church, Defense of Marriage Act, cabinet appointments, and exclusion of Christian leaders from religious events are clear proof that he has no respect for God, Christian values, or any reference to the value foundation that allowed the formation of our great country - The United States of America.

The Antichrist will be a 'man of peace' worshiped by millions, until the 'restrainer' is lifted. Then the real beast will show himself. Some consider it the time of Rapture when the Holy Spirit and the body of believers are removed, but that's not even the close answer. Remember who received world recognition for 'peace' without ever doing anything to earn it?

Revelation 13:6; "*And he opened his mouth in blasphemy against God, to blaspheme his name, and his tabernacle, and them that dwell in heaven.*"

Chapter 2

The War Against Christians

Verse 17: "And the dragon was wroth with the woman, and went to make war with the remnant of her seed, which keep the commandments of God, and have the testimony of Jesus Christ."

The War on The Remnant of Her Seed.

This is an article by Paul Marshall, CP Op-Ed Contributor, published on June 16, 2014. It describes the widespread war on 'the remnant of her seed.' Current-day Christians certainly are remnants of the seed of Christianity's beginning.

"For at least three reasons, the contemporary persecution of Christians demands attention: It is occurring on a massive scale, it is under reported, and in many parts of the world it is rapidly growing.

The Pew Forum on Religion and Public Life finds that Christians are suffering persecution in more places today than any other religious group; between 2006 and 2012, Pew says, they were targeted for harassment in 151 countries-three-quarters of the world's states. Similar findings are reported by the Vatican, Newsweek, the Economist, and the 60-year-old Christian support group Open Doors. Most people in the West are unaware of these facts, though that may be changing.

A few cases do get press coverage-the desperate plight of Meriam Ibrahim, for instance, who gave birth in a Sudanese prison just the other day. She was raised a Christian, but after officials learned that her long-absent father was a Muslim; she was sentenced to death for apostasy-for leaving Islam. And since in Sudan a Muslim woman may not be married to a Christian, her marriage to her American husband was declared void, and she was convicted of adultery and sentenced to 100 lashes to be administered before her execution. These punishments will be dropped if she renounces her Christian faith, which she steadfastly refuses to do.

Another case receiving attention is North Korea's sentencing of a South Korean missionary, Kim Jong-uk, to life with hard labor. On May 30, he was convicted of espionage and trying to start a church. North Korea also still holds Kenneth Bae, an American sentenced to 15 years' hard labor on charges of trying to use religion to overthrow the political system.

The Chinese government's demolition of the 3,000-member Sanjiang church in Wenzhou on April 28 was newsworthy partly because of the church's size, but also because Sanjiang was not an "underground" church but an official, approved, government-registered "Three-Self" church. Some 20 other official churches in the area have had all or parts of their buildings removed or demolished, and hundreds more are threatened with destruction.

And, most notorious, the abduction into slavery of hundreds of schoolgirls in Nigeria on April 14 by the al Qaeda-linked Boko Haram led news cycles and tweets for a time, though the religious dimensions of the story were often played down. While the kidnapped girls include Muslims (Boko Haram regards them as apostates because of their Western education), most are Christians, seized in a predominantly Christian area and now subjected to forced conversion.

These events get media attention because they are particularly poignant, or dramatic, or involve foreigners, but our media miss countless other stories. Since the kidnappings, Boko Haram has killed-not kidnaped, killed-hundreds of people, many in the predominantly Christian Gwoza area of Borno State, destroyed 36 churches, and kidnapped at least 8 more girls. On June 1, it attacked a Christian area in neighboring Adamawa state, killing 48 people.

In Sudan, a second woman, Faiza Abdalla, has been arrested on suspicion of converting to Christianity, and on April 8 a court terminated her marriage to a Catholic. Iran is imprisoning and torturing pastors from the rapidly growing house church movement, including an American citizen, Pastor Saeed Abedini.

Vietnam has imprisoned over 60 Christian leaders. Eritrea holds more than 1,000 Christians in conditions so inhumane that prisoner's die or are permanently crippled. In Somalia, in an ignored religious genocide, Al-Shabaab systematically hunts Christians and kills those it finds.

Of course, people of all religions suffer persecution for their faith or lack thereof-the situations of Baha'is and Jews in Iran, Ahmadis and Hindus in Pakistan, Tibetan Buddhists and Falun Gong in China, independent Buddhists in Vietnam, and Rohingya Muslims in Burma are particularly dire. Traditionally, the United States has been regarded as the country that advocates religious freedom for all, often to the disdain of other Westerners. In recent years, however, that has changed. Now America is quieter, while others speak up.

British prime minister David Cameron said recently that "our religion is now the most persecuted religion around the world" and "We should stand up against persecution of Christians and other religious groups wherever and whenever we can, and should be unashamed in doing so." German chancellor Angela Merkel has repeatedly stressed that Christians are the world's most widely persecuted religious group. Probably most outspoken of all is Vladimir Putin; no doubt this reflects geopolitical calculation, but the fact remains that he is stressing the matter.

The Italian Foreign Ministry has established an "Observatory on Religious Freedom." Quite properly, it is concerned with all religions, but its genesis was the upsurge in killings of Christians. Two years ago it hosted a conference on "Stopping the Massacre of Christians in Nigeria." Former French foreign minister Bernard Kouchner established a similar agency in the Quai d'Orsay, and later the ministry gave financial backing to an "Observatory of Cultural and Religious Pluralism" devoted to monitoring "attacks on freedom of conscience, on freedom of expression, and freedom of religion around the world," particularly with respect to the Arab Spring. Canada now has an ambassador-at-large for religious freedom, a title borrowed from the United States.

In the United States, meanwhile, the position of U.S. ambassador-at-large for religious freedom is vacant, as it has been for over half of President Barack Obama's tenure. Even when the position has been filled, in the last decade it has usually been marginalized.

President Obama gave a great speech on religious freedom at the National Prayer Breakfast, but little action followed. The United States has marginalized the issue in other ways, too.

After the massacre of 25 Copts by the Egyptian military on October 9, 2011, the White House lamented the "tragic loss of life among demonstrators and security forces" (emphasis added) and called for "restraint on all sides." As my colleague Sam Tadros commented, "I call upon the security forces to refrain from killing Christians, and upon Christians to refrain from dying."

On Easter morning in 2012, a church in Kaduna, Nigeria, was the target of a Boko Haram suicide car bombing that killed 39 and wounded dozens. (The previous Christmas, Boko Haram had bombed St. Theresa's Catholic Church outside the capital, Abuja, killing 44 worshipers, and also attacked churches in the towns of Jos, Kano, Gadaka, and Damaturu.) There was no official comment from the Obama administration about the Kaduna massacre on Christians' holiest day. Instead, Secretary of State Hillary Clinton issued a press release celebrating the Romani people and demanding that Europe become more inclusive of them.

At the beginning of the State Department's annual report on international religious freedom for 2013, Secretary of State John Kerry stated, "While Christians were a leading target of societal discrimination, abuse, and violence in some parts of the world, members of other religions, particularly Muslims, suffered as well." The assertion is incontrovertible, yet the wording elides the truth: Christians are not just "a leading target," they are the leading target. American officials seem so scared of being accused of selectively defending Christians that they consistently overcompensate and minimize what is happening.

The Catholic and Orthodox churches are more outspoken now than they were in the past, partly because the plight of their brethren, especially in the Middle East, is so stark. Pope Benedict XVI raised the issue many times. Pope Francis, speaking three days after the September 22, 2013, suicide bombing of All Saints Church in Peshawar, Pakistan, in which over 80 congregants were killed, urged Christians to examine their consciences about their response to anti-Christian persecution: "Am I indifferent to that, or does it affect me like it's a member of the family? Does it touch my heart, or doesn't it really affect me, [to know that] so many brothers and sisters in the family are giving their lives for Jesus Christ?"

Cardinal Timothy Dolan, in his November 11, 2013, address as he stepped down from chairing the U.S. Conference of Catholic Bishops, spoke of the "Via Crucis currently being walked by so many of our Christian brothers and sisters in other parts of the world, who are experiencing lethal persecution on a scale that defies belief."

Ecumenical Patriarch Bartholomew I of Constantinople has observed that "even the simple admission of Christian identity places the very existence of [the] faithful in daily threat," and Metropolitan Hilarion, chairman of the Russian Orthodox Church's Department for External Church Relations, has been raising the issue with American churches for several years.

Happily, there are signs that some Americans are again paying attention to the issue. Last month on Capitol Hill, a wide coalition of Christian leaders was convened by the co-chairs of the Religious Minorities in the Middle East Caucus, representatives Frank Wolf of Virginia, a Republican, and Anna Eshoo of California, a Democrat. They committed themselves to a "Pledge of Solidarity and Call to Action for Religious Freedom in the Middle East."

Although the persecution of Christians is widespread-Nigeria is where most are actually being killed, North Korea is the most repressive, China represses the largest number-the Pledge of Solidarity focuses on the Middle East and specifically on Syria, Iraq, and Egypt. These are countries where the situation has deteriorated rapidly to the point where Christian communities-along with smaller religious minorities such as Mandeans, Yezidis, Baha'is, and Ahmadis-now face "an existential threat to their presence in the lands where Christianity has its roots."

In the last decade, half of Iraq's Christians have fled the country, and many others have fled to the Kurdish region. In three days last August, Egypt's Coptic Christians experienced the worst single attack against their churches in 700 years-with 40 churches utterly destroyed and over 100 other sites severely damaged. Tens of thousands of Copts are estimated to have fled their homeland. Syria's Christians, like all Syrians, are caught in the middle of a brutal war, but, according to the pledge, they "are also victims of beheadings, summary executions, kidnappings, and forcible conversions, in deliberate efforts to suppress or eradicate their religious faith."

Too often these communities in the ancient heartland of Christianity have been forgotten. Speaking in Rome in December, Baghdad's Catholic Chaldean patriarch, Louis Sako, lamented, "We feel forgotten and isolated. We sometimes wonder, if they kill us all, what would be the reaction of Christians in the West? Would they do something then?"

In Washington, pledges like this new one tend to have about as much staying power as campaign promises. Still, there are reasons to believe that the Pledge of Solidarity will have an effect.

For one thing, the breadth of the coalition behind it is remarkable. Speakers included Cardinal Donald Wuerl, archbishop of Washington, Archbishop Oshagan Choloyan of the Armenian Apostolic Church of America, Leith Anderson, president of the National Association of Evangelicals, and Greek Orthodox Metropolitan Methodios of Boston. Pledge signers include Southern Baptist Ethics & Religious Liberty Commission president Russell D. Moore, Sojourners' Jim Wallis, Episcopal Church presiding bishop Katharine Jefferts Schori, Anglican Church in North America archbishop Robert Duncan, Samaritan's Purse president Franklin Graham, Robert George of Princeton University, chair of the U.S. Commission on International Religious Freedom, and George Marlin, chair of Aid to the Church in Need-USA.

Also promising is the fact that the Pledge of Solidarity sets forth focused goals-the appointment of a special envoy on Middle East religious minorities (legislation to create this position has passed the House but is stalled in the Senate, reportedly by a hold placed by Republican Tom Coburn of Oklahoma), a review of foreign aid to ensure it upholds principles of religious freedom, and an effort to see that refugee and reconstruction assistance reaches all religious communities.

But the pledge will have its greatest effect if, rather than falling on deaf ears, it awakens rank-and-file Americans and others to the religious diversity of the Middle East and the plight of Christians there and elsewhere. When Pope Francis and Ecumenical Patriarch Bartholomew I met in Jerusalem in May, their joint communiqué echoed the pledge, singling out "the Churches in Egypt, Syria, and

Iraq, which have suffered most grievously due to recent events."
The concern expressed by these religious leaders and a handful of
politicians is abundantly justified. Still missing is any large-scale
mobilization of free people on behalf of persecuted Christians
around the world." End of article.

Paul Marshall is senior fellow at the Hudson Institute's Center for
Religious Freedom and coauthor of Persecuted: The Global
Assault on Christians (Thomas Nelson, 2013). This column was
first published in The Weekly Standard.

7 Examples of Discrimination Against Christians in America.

John Hawkins at Townhall.com published the following article
September 17, 2013. It's titled: '7 Examples of Discrimination
Against Christians in America.'

"The majority of Americans are Christians, but we're not treated
with respect by the culture, the schools, or by our politicians.
"Vengeance" may be the Lord's to dish out, but that doesn't mean
Christians have to support the people who are attacking us or
meekly stand by when other followers of Christ are denigrated and
oppressed for their faith. The habitual wimpiness of so many
Christians is particularly grating because when Christians shine a
spotlight on these attacks and say, "That's enough," more often
than not we win. So, if Christians across the country were
consistently willing to speak out and take action, you'd be
surprised at how quickly our culture would begin to change. If that
happens, instead of seeing this many incidents every year (All of
these happened in 2013), they'd be a once in a blue moon
occurrence.

1) Florida Ministry Told To Choose Between Jesus And Helping

The Poor:"For the past 31 years, the Christian ministry has been providing food to the hungry in Lake City, Fla. without any problems. But all that changed when they said a state government worker showed up to negotiate a new contract. ...(A) state agriculture department official told them they would not be allowed to receive USDA food unless they removed portraits of Christ, the Ten Commandments, a banner that read 'Jesus is Lord' and stopping giving Bibles to the needy." When the government tells the Christian Service Center it has to give up on Christ or quit using USDA food to help the poor, that's religious discrimination.

2) Billy Graham Evangelistic Association: Obama's IRS Was "Targeting and Attempting to Intimidate Us:"It's well known that the IRS targeted Obama's political enemies in the Tea Party, but the IRS also targeted his Christian enemies in the Billy Graham Evangelistic Association.

Franklin Graham, the president of the Billy Graham Evangelistic Association and the family's international humanitarian organization Samaritan's Purse, said that the IRS notified the organizations in September that it was conducting a "review" of their activities for tax year 2010.

..."While these audits not only wasted taxpayer money, they wasted money contributed by donors for ministry purposes as we had to spend precious resources servicing the IRS agents in our offices," Graham wrote in the letter, which was shared with POLITICO. "I believe that someone in the administration was targeting and attempting to intimidate us. This is morally wrong and unethical – indeed some would call it 'un-American.'"

Graham said that "in light" of the IRS admission that it targeted tea party groups for added scrutiny, "I do not believe that the IRS audit of our two organizations last year is a coincidence – or justifiable."

The IRS would certainly deny targeting Graham's group because it's a Christian organization, but of course, the IRS would deny that it targeted the Tea Party groups for political reasons as well.

3) California Christians Found "Not Guilty" of Reading Bible Near Government Offices:"A court has said that a pair of Christians were 'allowed' to read the Bible aloud outside the Department of Motor Vehicles in Hemet, California. Wasn't it kind of the government courts in California to say that these Christians were allowed to have their rights to free religious expression? ...Back in 2011 Mark Mackey and Bret Coronado were arrested and charged with misdemeanor offenses for reading the Bible outside the DMV location. ... But on August 13, Superior Court Judge Timothy Freer found the men 'not guilty' of any offenses. ...Interestingly, the judge also pointed out that the law prosecutors tried to invoke was likely unconstitutional as it gave law enforcement overbroad powers to quash public gatherings in the first place. Sadly, this case did not go toward settling the constitutionality of the law, but it was a victory of sorts to have the judge even mention the fact."

Yes, there were actually Americans arrested for reading the Bible on public property. What do you think the chances are that two Muslims reading the Quran would have been arrested under the same circumstances?

4) Colorado Baker Faces Year In Jail For Refusing To Make Cake For Gay Wedding: You can support gay marriage or you can be Christian, but you can't do both. You can pretend to do both, but you're giving up your Christian beliefs to be more palatable to

people who are hostile to Christianity. The folks at Masterpiece Cakeshop simply declined to make a cake for a gay wedding because it conflicted with their Christian beliefs. They learned that's now illegal.

According to attorney Nicolle Martin, the owners of a Colorado bakery could face a year in prison for refusing to make a cake for a gay wedding, Jim Hoft reported at the Gateway Pundit Monday.

"The complainants can sue him civilly in the regular courts system or he can potentially be prosecuted by the district attorney for up to twelve months in jail," Martin told Hoft.

In June, the Advocate said the Colorado Attorney General's office filed a discrimination complaint against the owners of Masterpiece Cakeshop in Denver after the bakers refused to bake a cake for Dave Mullins and Charlie Craig, a Denver area gay couple, last year.

But Jack Phillips, one of the owners, declined to make the cake citing his Christian beliefs.

"We would close down the bakery before we compromised our beliefs," he told KCNC, adding that protests and petitions will not make him change his mind.

We have Americans being threatened with jail time for doing nothing more than refusing to affirmatively sanction an event that goes against Christianity. In other words, liberals aren't just trying to make gay marriage legal; they're trying to make opposition to gay marriage illegal.

5) Air Force Veteran Faces A Court Martial For Opposing Gay

Marriage: Under Barack Obama, the military has become aggressively anti-Christian and pro-gay to such an extent that the troops are no longer even allowed to privately oppose gay marriage.

Senior Master Sgt. Phillip Monk found himself at odds with his Lackland Air Force Base commander after he objected to her plans to severely punish an instructor who had expressed religious objections to homosexuality. During the conversation, his commander ordered him to share his personal views on homosexuality.

"I was relieved of my position because I don't agree with my commander's position on gay marriage," he told me. "We've been told that if you publicly say that homosexuality is wrong, you are in violation of Air Force policy."

...Last week, Monk was supposed to meet with an Air Force investigator tasked with gathering facts about the complaint. But when he arrived, Monk was immediately read his Miranda Rights and accused of providing false statements in a conversation Monk had with (Fox's Todd Starnes).

After he was relieved of his duties, the Liberty Institute filed a religious discrimination complaint on his behalf. ..."I immediately got the sense that this was retaliation against me for coming forward with my religious discrimination complaint," he said.

The accusations against Monk are a court-martial offense in the Air Force – and it's quite possible that the 19-year veteran with a spotless record could be booted out of the military because of his Christian beliefs. And he's not the only Christian at Lackland Air Force Base facing persecution for opposing gay marriage, according to Monk's pastor.

If you think the military has problems recruiting soldiers now, let the military keep persecuting Christians for their faith and see how well it does over the long haul. Of course, that wouldn't upset the Left one bit, but the rest of us should be concerned.

6) Government Forces Churches To Get Permits For Baptisms: Nevertheless, the Park Service recently began a new policy requiring churches that wished to hold baptisms in public waters to apply for a special permit at least 48 hours in advance of the baptism. The Park Service justified this recent demand by saying that the permits were necessary to "maintain park natural/cultural resources and quality visitor experiences, specific terms and conditions have been established."

...On August 21, Rep. Jason Smith (Missouri, R) heeded the complaints of his constituents and wrote a letter to the NPS asking what the heck was going on...

...Between citizen outrage and Rep. Smith's threat to bring the matter before the full Congress, however, the Park Service quickly reversed its new policy, writing to the Congressman that, "As of today, the park's policy has been clarified to state that no permit will be required for baptisms within the Riverways. I can assure you the National Park Service has no intention of limiting the number of baptisms performed within the park."

When the government demands that a church get a permit to do baptisms, it's also tacitly saying it has the right to deny that permit. That's not acceptable.

7) Florida Professor Demands Student Stomp On Jesus: It all

started with a conflict between an antagonistic professor and one brave student at Florida Atlantic University. Ryan Rotela was told by his professor to write Jesus Christ's name on a piece of paper and stomp on it. Rotela defiantly refused and in retaliation, a formal disciplinary action was started against him.

But, before the system could roll over Rotela, a funny thing happened. The word about what was happening to him got out, Christians became outraged, and suddenly the university's tune quickly changed. "FAU's Senior Vice President for Student Affairs, Dr. Charles Brown, has since issued a groveling formal apology." Next thing you know, the disciplinary action was waved off.

Now, comes word that the professor, Deandre Poole, has been put on administrative leave following a withering public response, that included complaints from the Governor of Florida, Rick Scott.

Unfortunately, that story didn't have a happy ending. Even after the governor got involved, Deandre Poole still kept his job. However, had Christians not risen up, the student who refused to stomp on Jesus would have been the one punished while the professor would have paid no price at all. Moreover, you can be sure there won't be any more Jesus stomping going on in the classrooms at Florida Atlantic University any time soon.

If there's a lesson here, it's that when Christians refuse to back down, we usually win. What that means is if enough Christians stand up for our faith, you'll be surprised how fast the people in power lose their nerve about going after us. End of article.

Turkey's Christians Under Siege

This next article is By John Eibner, Middle East Quarterly, Spring 2011. It's titled: Turkey's Christians Under Siege

"The brutal murder of the head of Turkey's Catholic Church, Bishop Luigi Padovese, on June 3, 2010, has rattled the country's small, diverse, and hard-pressed Christian community. The 62-year-old bishop, who spearheaded the Vatican's efforts to improve Muslim-Christian relations in Turkey, was stabbed repeatedly at his Iskenderun home by his driver and bodyguard Murat Altun, who concluded the slaughter by decapitating Padovese and shouting, "I killed the Great Satan. Allahu Akhbar!" He then told the police that he had acted in obedience to a "command from God."

The brutal murder on June 3, 2010, of the head of Turkey's Catholic church, Bishop Luigi Padovese, was seen in 2006 leading the funeral procession of another slain priest, Andrea Santoro, was met by denials and obfuscation—not only by the Turkish authorities but also by Western governments and even the Vatican.

Though bearing all the hallmarks of a jihadist execution, the murder was met by denials and obfuscation—not only by the Turkish authorities but also by Western governments and the Vatican. This is not wholly surprising. In the post-9/11 era, it has become commonplace to deny connections between Islam and acts of violence despite much evidence to the contrary. But while this denial has undoubtedly sought to win the hearts and minds of Muslims, as opposed to Christians, Jews, or any other religious group, it has served to encourage Islamist terrorism and to exacerbate the persecution of non-Muslim minorities even in the most secularized Muslim states.

For all President Barack Obama's high praise for its "strong, vibrant, secular democracy," and Prime Minister Recep Tayyip Erdoğan's "Alliance of Civilizations" rhetoric, Turkey is very much entrenched in the clash of civilizations paradigm. Unless Ankara is prepared to combat the widespread "Christophobia" that fuels violence and other forms of repression, the country's Christians are doomed to remain an oppressed and discriminated against minority, and Turkey's aspirations of democratic transformation and full integration with Europe will remain stillborn.

The Victim and His Mission

Consecrated bishop in November 2004, half a year following Cardinal Joseph Ratzinger's elevation to the papacy, Padovese belonged to the body of intellectually sharp, proactive clerics who share Benedict XVI's ecumenical understanding of the church and its global mission of evangelization, especially in the Islamic Middle East where a century of intensive de-Christianization now threatens the faith's regional existence.

Padovese's mission in Turkey was to help save the country's Christian community from extinction and to create conditions for its religious and cultural renaissance. Rejecting the church's historic dhimmi status as a protected religious minority under Islam—which reduced it to little more than a submissive worshipping agency with no other legitimate activity—he viewed Turkey's European Union candidacy as a golden opportunity for winning significant concessions from Ankara and pinned high hopes on the Special Assembly for the Middle East of the Synod of Bishops, which took place in Rome in October 2010. However, the synod ended on a sour note. While confirming the Second Vatican Council's positive shift in attitude toward Judaism and unequivocal rejection of anti-Semitism, the Middle Eastern bishops sought to enhance the security of their flocks by playing an anti-Israel card and criticizing Israel—the one country of the region with a growing Christian population—with a directness that was not employed in relation to any Islamic state, no matter how repressive.

Had it not been for his murder, the bishop would have traveled to meet the pope in Cyprus on the very next day for the launch of the synod's Instrumentum laboris, the Vatican's strategic plan for reviving Christianity in its Middle Eastern cradle, to which Padovese was a substantial contributor.

Chapter 3

More War on Christians

Boko Haram in Nigeria

Following is an article by Leonardo Blair, reporter at christianpost.com, May 16, 2014:

Abubakar Shekau, leader of the Islamic militant group Boko Haram, has made it clear that the recent abduction of nearly 300 mostly Christian schoolgirls in Nigeria is not merely about denying education to women but a war against the damaging effects of Christians and Christianity in Nigeria.

In a translation of a nearly 1-hour video by Sahara Reporters, he explained how wars were waged against countries like Iraq and Afghanistan in the name of Christianity and now there is a plan in motion to do the same in Nigeria.

"Here is what Bush once said and we will repeat it here. He said all the fights going on in Iraq and Afghanistan are Christian war, crusade, it is a known issue. And that they will crush Afghanistan, today I will say my own," said Shekau.

"To the people of the world, everybody should know his status, it is either you are with us Mujahedeen or you are with the Christians. The likes of Obama, Lincoln, Clinton, Jonathan, Aminu Kano. They are your fathers of democracy, the likes of Tafawa Balewa. It is Usman Dan Fodiyo that is our own," he continued.

"We know what is happening in this world, it is a Jihad war against Christians and Christianity. It is a war against western education, democracy and constitution," he said.

Shekau said despite the international outcry over the abduction of Nigerian schoolgirls, the Jihad hasn't even started in Nigeria yet.

"We have not started, next time we are going inside Abuja; we are going to refinery and town of Christians. Do you know me? I have no problem with Jonathan. This is what I know in Quran. This is a war against Christians and democracy and their constitution, Allah says we should finish them when we get them," he said.

He said Nigerian politicians consorting with western leaders in the name of progress and development is apostasy.

"You are sitting down in the name of clerics with turbans; you are sitting with Christians thinking it is mediation. Saying it is development and progress, what progress after you have deviated from Allah? We will die killing and slaughtering them, if you meet infidels in battle field brethren, just harvest their necks; Allah said it and not Shekau," he noted.

He then ripped into human rights groups for promoting homosexuality.

"And you are saying you are advocates of human rights. Humor sexual people like you, promoters of same sex marriage, animals knows rights more than them, even sheep doesn't sleep [with] sheep, but you keep a woman and a woman as husband and wife," he said. End of Article.

Is there a war against Christians in America?

The conservative.info published another article about the war titled: "Is there a war against Christians in America?"

On the surface war seems like a harsh word to apply to what we are beginning to see more and more of in the press, on the news and in the courts. War is the attempt to destroy and subdue what one considers its enemy. This "war" is not being waged against any other religion. It seems like these groups that are waging this "war" are more than willing to embrace any other religion as long as it does not name the name of Christianity. Anything that bears the name of Christ or relates to Christ in any way is legal game for their attacks. I could go into detail about the attacks against the Ten Commandments, Christmas, manger scenes, and on and on and on.

The very real and present danger lies in greater agendas though. These groups that are attacking Christianity have a deeper and far more sinister reason for their attacks. One reason for these attacks is that Christianity is in direct opposition to the open sinfulness some people want America to embrace. As long as America stands on Judea/Christian law, groups like sodomite's and lesbians will not be free to spread their poison across America. Organizations like NAMBLA (North American Man Boy Love Association) will always have their hands tied from pursuing their perverse lifestyles of seducing children. Political organizations like socialist (they hate Christianity), Feminist (They see Christianity as constrictive), left wing Democrats (Christianity is a burden) and others for political reasons are in support of eliminating Christianity from America. Religious groups that do not embrace Christianity such as the occult (A vastly growing community), Wicca (A very strong witchcraft community), Atheism (disavow God's existence), Satanism (worshippers of Satan), secularist (man is his own deity), Islam (worshippers of Allah (they hate Christianity and refer to us as infidels and dogs)), and others too many to list in their total number, all feel like they are strong enough together to destroy Christianity in America. Together and separately, these groups fight to chip away at Christian liberty, using liberal left wing sympathetic courts to advance their attacks. These people have a hatred for Christianity that is fueled by Satan himself. Every time a left wing judge who is sympathetic to them gets on the bench they get stronger.

The other focus is an idealistic and political desire to have the world come together in one mind and spirit of working together for what is called the betterment of all of mankind without God. These people see religion as the source of all the worlds evil. They blame most wars on religion and they are right. The problem is that they place true Christianity in this group and nothing could be further from the truth. Perverted Christianity by people who have private agendas and an anti-Semitic mindset use Christianity to further their ends just like they use any convenient vessel to spread their hate. The people who believe this are blind to the truth and they do not want to see how Christianity has been used by corrupt people.   These groups believe man is his own God. John Lennon who was a member of the communist party spoke of this in his song "Imagine". This song was written to promote a world without God, heaven or hell. This song could be an anthem for communism and people embraced the song like it was the greatest thing that ever came along. It received accolades for greatness and the song was a slap in the face to democracy and Christianity.

Some have called this mindset that is working to bring the world together in one accord "The one world order". Some of you will laugh at that. Laugh on, but read on please. Many of you have seen logos and different things at work depicting this mindset, even if you did not recognize it for what it was. The company I worked for had these. One was a screen saver they encouraged everyone to install on their company computers. They also have it in printed form that can be posted around the plant. It started out with the company logo in the center of the screen and then sentences began coming outward from the logo. These sentences were comprised of statements such as "One World", "One Team", "One Mind", "One Goal", "One Thought", "One Voice", etc. Christianity is the only religion in the world that distinctly teaches against and has dire warnings concerning this order. Christianity relates this time to a world leader that will bring the entire world together for a brief time in a peace and prosperity like the world has never seen. This leader will be hailed as the true Messiah. All of the world will flock to his banner. This peace will only be a short lived one though. His leadership will usher in a time of violence and war like the world has never seen.

This makes Christianity a direct opposing force to the completion of these groups goals for a world united together for the benefit of all mankind as one people. These left wing groups are activists working toward this goal. On the surface this seems like a wonderful idea. Who would not want the world to come together working together with one mind and one goal. There are far too many reasons to go into in this article why this will not work according to Christianity. Christian ministers have been preaching about this world order and the reasons it will not work for centuries. The Bible has a lot to say about this time called "the end times".

These left wing activists do want a financially strong America and a unified America, just not a conservative or a conservative Christian America. For years now, these left wing groups have been wanting to destroy anything that strengthens America and unifies us as a conservative or a Christian nation. They have attacked relentlessly everyone from Columbus to the founding fathers to any other person or event that traditional Americans admire and look up to. They have tried to change history concerning the siege of the Alamo. They have tried to show the founding fathers in a cruel and vicious light. They make sure they remind you that Thomas Jefferson owned slaves and had children by them. They do not tell you that it was the accepted norm of the time. It is just a way they throw dirt at the founding fathers.

This traditional mindset which is grounded in Christianity must be destroyed before the United States will be open minded enough to be a true member of a "One Mind, One World, One Team, One Thought", One Voice" order.

These same people recently tried to smear and ridicule a great American president (Ronald Reagan). They know they cannot reach the older Americans who have been brought up in patriotic pride. They want to infiltrate the education system, courts and media to supplant their poisonous rhetoric into the next generation of Americans.

Christian morality and traditions is what has made America the light and strength of freedom for all the world to see.

They have a hatred for the grass roots traditions that made America great that burns with an unquenchable fire. This same fire of hatred is what makes them hate George W. Bush like they do. They see their agendas set back with every day that he spends in the White House and they are like ravenous dogs in their unrelenting and deceitful attacks against him. I believe their hatred is so strong they would even challenge the Constitution itself to get him out of office. I hear some of these left wing liberal Bush haters on TV and I (God forbid) get the idea sometimes that they are anxiously waiting to see another attack against America by terrorist so it will give them ammunition to use against him. Television cannot hide the fire of hatred that you can see in their eyes when they speak about him.

They have a burning hatred for Christian morality and traditions that has made America the light and strength of freedom. They want an America that is free from conservative tradition. They want an America where sin is not defined by Christian morality. They want an America free from restraints upon their actions. They want an America not hobbled by Christian codes of ethics. These groups want the rule of law to be "anything goes". They want an America that does not remind them that they have moral responsibility. These left wing groups feel like they have to break the hold Christianity has on America in order for their goals to be achieved.

Some of these left wing groups would embrace with enthusiasm an America more socialist in its politics and reforms. They want the people to depend on the government to supply people's every need and want. This gives them power over the people. They do not want people to accept responsibility for their own actions or their future. They want the government to be the people's security blanket against losing their lifestyle. If the people fall on hard times, they want a government that is there to tell them what went wrong and to bail them out. They want people to get so dependent on the government that they cry out like a spoiled child "I deserve better and you (the government) owe it to me". This puts the government in control and the people as dependents.

The founding fathers had a different plan. Their plan was for the government to be controlled by and answerable to "We the people". Liberal left wing activist want to change that. They feel like they know what is best for the people. They want the people answerable to the government. I feel like they would change the Constitution From "We the people, in order to form a more perfect union", to read "We the government, in order to form a more perfect union".

Yes, there is a war against Christianity. There is a war against the grass roots traditions of our founding fathers. There is a war against an America governed by law founded on Christian morality and principles. There is a war against the family unit as defined by Christianity.

There is a war for what the future of America is going to be. The lines are drawn in this war and they are divisive. You are a participant in this war whether you want to be or not. You can be a victim or an open soldier in this war against Christianity. One thing is certain though. You and your children will be affected severely by the outcome of this war. You cannot stand on the sidelines hoping it will not affect you. You may remain silent and hope it will go away but you will then be a silent victim of this war.

If you do not go to the polls and vote, you are casting a vote for the candidate you do not agree with because of your abstinence. If you do not get involved in this war against Christianity, you are lending support for the enemies of Christianity by your silence! End of Article.

The World's War on Christians

This is an article by Robert J. Morgan at huffingtonpost.com, dated March 16, 2014, titled: "The World's War on Christians."

Last spring, I was having supper with Christian workers who had devoted their lives to North Africa. They were retired missionaries. I left the table to take a call from a reporter. He wanted my opinion on the subject of the persecution of Christians, claiming many of his sources in the media and academia were downplaying accounts of Christian persecution, both past and present. I gave a few comments, then returned to my companions who were in mid-story, telling one account after another of the devastation occurring in their former areas on labor -- churches burned, Christians killed, believers fired from jobs, church members imprisoned, leaders slain.

I thought to myself, anyone who downplays the persecution of Christians is deeply mistaken.

Baroness Warsi, a government official in Great Britain and a Muslim, recently warned that Christian populations are "hemorrhaging" in nations like Pakistan, where persecution against believers is intense and sustained. In many places Christianity is in danger of extinction because of cold-blooded, systematic slaughter.

In his new book, 'The Global War on Christians,' John L. Allen, Jr., senior Vatican correspondent for the National Catholic Report, called the massive worldwide wave of anti-Christian violence "the most dramatic religion story of the early 21st century."

He wrote, "Christians today indisputably are the most persecuted religious body on the face of the planet, and too often their new martyrs suffer in silence."

This is a human rights disaster of epic proportions, claimed Allen, and "the world's best-kept secret." While it's true attacks are mounting against adherents of other faiths, 80 percent of all acts of religious discrimination in the world today are directed at Christians.

The worst killings may be in Northern Nigeria. According to the watchdog agency Open Doors, more Christians were killed in Northern Nigeria last year than in the rest of the world combined. Christian women are forced at knifepoint to convert to Islam, and the Nigerian terrorist group Boko Haram is seeking to eradicate Christianity.

In Iran, where Christianity has been growing despite persecution, Pastor Behnam Irani has now passed the 900th day in prison for his faith. Another pastor, Saeed Abedini, incarcerated in Tehran's Evin Prison for his faith, is denied needed medications for injuries sustained at the hands of guards. On October 30, a Christian in Iran was flogged for taking communion.

Reports from Iraq tell of over a million Christians put to flight there. The number of known Christians inside Iraq has been reduced from 1.5 million to around 200,000.

A woman named Wehazit Berhane Debesai is the 25th known person to die for Christ in the wretched prisons of Eritrea, where several thousand people are behind bars because of their faith. But the phrase "behind bars" is a misnomer. At the Me'eter Prison in the Eritrean desert, inmates, mostly Christians, are held in large metal storage containers that become ovens by day and freezers by night where dehydrated victims drink their own sweat and urine to stay alive.

John L. Allen, Jr. asks logical questions when he wonders why there's so much outrage over Abu Ghraib and Guantanamo, when the plight of Christians at Me'eter is never mentioned in the press. Indeed in every Muslim-dominated land, Christians are oppressed -- even in moderate states like Turkey. The Arab Spring has become a Christian Winter in places like Egypt where the Coptic church is facing dire and dangerous days.

Christians are faring no better under Communism. North Korea remains the most evil nation on earth due to the oppression of its people, especially Christians. According to accounts, 80 people were machine-gunned the other day in a stadium in front of 10,000 people. The crime for some of the victims was owning a Bible. Reports from North Korea have told of Christians being pulverized by steamrollers. Hundreds of thousands of believers north of the Thirty-Eight Parallel have simply vanished. At this very moment, there are over 50,000 Christians suffering in concentration camps in Korea.

Turning elsewhere, Christians in India are trying to resist discriminatory laws promoted by Hindu extremists. In the Indian state of Orissa, as many as 500 Christians were hacked to death some time ago, with thousands more injured or left homeless. As many as 350 churches were destroyed. Just last month, the body of a boy named Anmoi was recovered in North India. He had been tortured and murdered, evidently because he had gone to Sunday School. His face was burned, his mouth tied shut, his toes broken, his stomach scalded with hot coals, then he had been drowned. He was only seven-years-old.

In Burma, the government has launched helicopter strikes against Christian regions of the country, with soldiers authorized to kill followers of Christ on sight. Christians in the Central Africa Republic are also systematically targeted for violence.

According to Open Doors, the most dangerous countries in the world for Christian are, in order of horror: North Korea, Afghanistan, Saudi Arabia, Somalia, Iran, Maldives, Uzbekistan, Yemen, Iraq, Pakistan, Eritrea, Laos, Nigeria, Mauritania, Egypt, Sudan, Bhutan, Turkmenistan, Vietnam, Chechnya, and China.

It's hard to estimate the number of Christians who die each year from martyrdom. Open Doors was able to verify 1200 deaths in 2012, but the true number is much higher. Indeed, the Center for the Study of Global Christianity at Gordon-Conwell estimated a million Christians were martyred in between 2000 and 2010.

If much of the media hasn't yet realized the significance of this story, the Bible anticipated it years ago. The founder of Christianity, after all, was tortured to death and his original 12 followers were all persecuted; most were slain. Though his message was a Gospel of peace, his critics nailed him to a cross but failed to keep him in the tomb. They hated him but could not contain him. They sought to limit his influence, but they only broadened his impact. End of Article.

Global War on Christians

Following is an article by Catholicnewsagency.com about John L. Allen's book, titled: "Global War on Christians."

Denver, Colo., Oct 6, 2013 / 04:06 pm (CNA).- In his new book "The Global War on Christians," Vatican analyst John Allen, Jr. details anti-Christian abuse worldwide, drawing light to the tremendous scale of violence against the world's most persecuted religion.

"I don't think it takes any religious convictions or confessional interests at all to see that defense of persecuted Christians deserves to be the world's number one human rights priority," Allen, a noted Vatican journalist and author, told CNA in an Oct. 2 interview.

"You didn't have to be Jewish in the '70s to be worried about dissident Jews in the Soviet Union; you didn't have to be black in the '80s to be concerned about apartheid in South Africa; and you equally don't have to be Christian today to recognize that Christians are the most persecuted religious body on the planet."

Allen's work, published Tuesday by Image Books, arises directly from a conversation he had with Cardinal Dolan in 2009, in which the prelate made the point that Christians "need to do a better job of telling these stories" of Christian persecution, like the body of "Holocaust literature" showed the suffering of Jews under Hitler.

However, Allen became interested in the subject of anti-Christian persecution while traveling to Ukraine for Pope John Paul II's 2001 trip there.

At that time, Allen met the granddaughter of an Eastern Catholic priest who had been killed in a gulag during the Soviet era.

"That conversation brought home that martyrdom is very much a feature of the contemporary Christian landscape."

Prior to that, he said, "like a lot of Catholics ... when I thought of martyrdom, I considered it an artifact of the early centuries of the Church, the early Christian martyrs under Nero and Diocletian."

"The more I would travel the world and meet victims of anti-Christian persecution in various places, the more the scale and scope of this thing came home to me."

Allen notes that throughout the first decade of the 21st century, 100,000 Christians were killed per year – 11 new martyrs every hour – and secular human rights groups estimate that 80 percent of religious freedom violations are current directed against Christians.

Despite these massive figures, the worldwide persecution of Christians is little known in the U.S., and Allen said the first purpose of his book is "to end the silence about anti-Christian persecution ... to put it on the map."

Highlighting that "this is a literal war against Christians on a global scale," involving direct physical violence, harassment, and imprisonment, Allen works in the book to chronicle persecution against Christians in Africa, Asia, Latin America, the Middle East, and eastern Europe.

Having done that, Allen then clarified several myths about Christian persecution, such as the claims that no one saw the persecution coming; the issue is solely a political one; and "it's all about Islam."

While acknowledging that "we can't be naïve" about the fact that quite "a fair share of Christian suffering around the world" is related to radical forms of Islam, Allen said that "it does an injustice to Christian victims of persecution ... as a result of other forces, to leave them out of the picture simply because their oppressors aren't Muslims."

He noted that recently, "the most violent anti-Christian pogrom anywhere was in India," and at the hands of radical Hindus. "I don't think it's fair to those Indian victims to forget them simply because they don't have the politically appropriate enemy."

Allen chose to distinguish between the physically violent persecution of Christians around the world –including churches being blown up in Pakistan or tens of thousands of Christians languishing in concentration camps in North Korea – and the "separate, but related" issue of a secularist movement in the Western world which discourages the expression of all religions.

He hopes that his book will help broaden the view of many people in the United States, to see that "there are real lethal threats to religious freedom out there that need our attention, too."

The second major purpose of the book, Allen explained, is "to galvanize people, Christians particularly, to take action. I don't want people just to be aware of (Christian persecution), I want them to do something about it."

While many Americans learning of Christian persecution in far-off places might feel powerless to stop it, or even to assist its victims, Allen uses the final part of his book to explain the consequences and responses appropriate to the issue.

Some of the response can be "broad policy" of the government, "big picture level" decisions: giving preference to victims of anti-Christian violence in refugee resettlement policy, and paying attention to the voices of Syrians saying that to seek regime change in their country would be quite harmful to them, he said.

"But there are things that people can do on a smaller scale, without waiting to live in a different world," he added.

In particular, Allen suggested donating to the Catholic Near East Welfare Association, which provides "basic food and medical care to Christian refugees from Syria."

A "feasible financial contribution" for a middle-class American can do much to help Christians who have fled Syria, he said, "and it's a direct way of saving the lives of Christians who are today the world's most persecuted religious body."

"There are ways in which individuals can effect change," he concluded.

"So don't feel powerless, don't feel that this is a tragedy we can do nothing about, because there are steps we can take." End of Article.

Chapter 4

America's Most Biblically-Hostile U.S. President

The following article was published by David Barton at Wallbuilders.com on April 30, 2014. It's titled: 'America's Most Biblically-Hostile U.S. President.' The numbers 1-92 in brackets identify the source of the comment at the end of the article:

"When one observes President Obama's unwillingness to accommodate America's four-century long religious conscience protection through his attempts to require Catholics to go against their own doctrines and beliefs, one is tempted to say that he is anti-Catholic. But that characterization would not be correct. Although he has recently singled out Catholics, he has equally targeted traditional Protestant beliefs over the past four years. So since he has attacked Catholics and Protestants, one is tempted to say that he is anti-Christian. But that, too, would be inaccurate.

He has been equally disrespectful in his appalling treatment of religious Jews in general and Israel in particular. So perhaps the most accurate description of his antipathy toward Catholics,

Protestants, religious Jews, and the Jewish nation would be to characterize him as anti-Biblical. And then when his hostility toward Biblical people of faith is contrasted with his preferential treatment of Muslims and Muslim nations, it further strengthens the accuracy of the anti-Biblical descriptor. In fact, there have been numerous clearly documented times when his pro-Islam positions have been the cause of his anti-Biblical actions.

Listed below in chronological order are (1) numerous records of his attacks on Biblical persons or organizations; (2) examples of the hostility toward Biblical faith that have become evident in the past three years in the Obama-led military; (3) a listing of his open attacks on Biblical values; and finally (4) a listing of numerous incidents of his preferential deference for Islam's activities and positions, including letting his Islamic advisors guide and influence his hostility toward people of Biblical faith. The bracketed number at the end of each item is the reference at the end of the article.

1. Acts of hostility toward people of Biblical faith:

December 2009-Present - The annual White House Christmas cards, rather than focusing on Christmas or faith, instead highlight things such as the family dogs. And the White House Christmas tree ornaments include figures such as Mao Tse-Tung and a drag queen. [1]

June 2013 – The Obama Department of Justice defunds a Young Marines chapter in Louisiana because their oath mentioned God, and another youth program because it permits a voluntary student-led prayer. [2]

February 2013 – The Obama Administration announces that the

rights of religious conscience for individuals will not be protected under the Affordable Care Act. [3]

January 2013 – Pastor Louie Giglio is pressured to remove himself from praying at the inauguration after it is discovered he once preached a sermon supporting the Biblical definition of marriage. [4]

February 2012 – The Obama administration forgives student loans in exchange for public service, but announces it will no longer forgive student loans if the public service is related to religion. [5]

January 2012 – The Obama administration argues that the First Amendment provides no protection for churches and synagogues in hiring their pastors and rabbis. [6]

December 2011 – The Obama administration denigrates other countries' religious beliefs as an obstacle to radical homosexual rights. [7]

November 2011 – President Obama opposes inclusion of President Franklin Roosevelt's famous D-Day Prayer in the WWII Memorial. [8]

November 2011 – Unlike previous presidents, Obama studiously avoids any religious references in his Thanksgiving speech. [9]

August 2011 – The Obama administration releases its new health care rules that override religious conscience protections for medical workers in the areas of abortion and contraception. [10]

April 2011 – For the first time in American history, Obama urges passage of a non-discrimination law that does not contain hiring protections for religious groups, forcing religious organizations to hire according to federal mandates without regard to the dictates of their own faith, thus eliminating conscience protection in hiring. [11]

February 2011 – Although he filled posts in the State Department, for more than two years Obama did not fill the post of religious freedom ambassador, an official that works against religious persecution across the world; he filled it only after heavy pressure from the public and from Congress. [12]

January 2011 – After a federal law was passed to transfer a WWI Memorial in the Mojave Desert to private ownership, the U. S. Supreme Court ruled that the cross in the memorial could continue to stand, but the Obama administration refused to allow the land to be transferred as required by law, and refused to allow the cross to be re-erected as ordered by the Court. [13]

November 2010 – Obama misquotes the National Motto, saying it is "E pluribus unum" rather than "In God We Trust" as established by federal law. [14]

October 19, 2010 – Obama begins deliberately omitting the phrase about "the Creator" when quoting the Declaration of Independence – an omission he has made on no less than seven occasions. [15]

May 2009 – Obama declines to host services for the National Prayer Day (a day established by federal law) at the White House. [16]

April 2009 – When speaking at Georgetown University, Obama orders that a monogram symbolizing Jesus' name be covered when he is making his speech. [17]

April 2009 – In a deliberate act of disrespect, Obama nominated three pro-abortion ambassadors to the Vatican; of course, the pro-life Vatican rejected all three. [18]

February 2009 – Obama announces plans to revoke conscience protection for health workers who refuse to participate in medical activities that go against their beliefs, and fully implements the plan in February 2011. [19]

April 2008 – Obama speaks disrespectfully of Christians, saying they "cling to guns or religion" and have an "antipathy to people who aren't like them." [20]

2. Acts of hostility from the Obama-led military toward people of Biblical faith:

December 2013 - A naval facility required that two nativity scenes -- scenes depicting the event that caused Christmas to be declared a national federal holiday -- be removed from the base dining hall and be confined to the base chapel, thus disallowing the open public acknowledgment of this national federal holiday. [21]

December 2013 - An Air Force base that allowed various public displays ordered the removal of one simply because it contained religious content. [22]

October 2013 – A counter-intelligence briefing at Fort Hood tells soldiers that evangelical Christians are a threat to Americans and that for a soldier to donate to such a group "was punishable under military regulations." [23]

October 2013 – Catholic priests hired to serve as military chaplains are prohibited from performing Mass services at base chapels during the government financial shutdown. When they offered to freely do Mass for soldiers, without regard to whether or not the chaplains were receiving pay, they are still denied permission to do so. [24]

October 2013 - The Air Force Academy, in response to a complaint from Mikey Weinstein's Military Religious Freedom Foundation, makes "so help me God" optional in cadets' honor oath. [25]

August 2013 - A Department of Defense military training manual teaches soldiers that people who talk about "individual liberties, states' rights, and how to make the world a better place" are "extremists." It also lists the Founding Fathers -- those "colonists who sought to free themselves from British rule" -- as examples of those involved in "extremist ideologies and movements." [26]

August 2013 - A Senior Master Sergeant was removed from his position and reassigned because he told his openly lesbian squadron commander that she should not punish a staff sergeant who expressed his views in favor of traditional marriage. [27]

August 2013 - The military does not provide heterosexual couples specific paid leave to travel to a state just for the purpose of being married, but it did extend these benefits to homosexual couples who want to marry, thus giving them preferential treatment not available to heterosexuals. [28]

August 2013 - The Air Force, in the midst of having launched a series of attacks against those expressing traditional religious or moral views, invited a drag queen group to perform at a base. [29]

July 2013 - When an Air Force sergeant with years of military service questioned a same-sex marriage ceremony performed at the Air Force Academy's chapel, he received a letter of reprimand telling him that if he disagreed, he needed to get out of the military. His current six-year re-enlistment was then reduced to only one-year, with the notification that he "be prepared to retire at the end of this year." [30]

July 2013 - An Air Force chaplain who posted a website article on the importance of faith and the origin of the phrase "There are no atheists in foxholes" was officially ordered to remove his post because some were offended by the use of that famous World War II phrase. [31]

June 2013 - The U. S. Air Force, in consultation with the Pentagon, removed an inspirational painting that for years has been hanging at Mountain Home Air Force Base because its title was "Blessed Are The Peacemakers" -- a phrase from Matthew 5:9 in the Bible. [32]

June 2013 – The Obama administration "strongly objects" to a Defense Authorization amendment to protect the constitutionally-guaranteed religious rights of soldiers and chaplains, claiming that it would have an "adverse effect on good order, discipline, morale, and mission accomplishment." [33]

June 2013 – At a joint base in New Jersey, a video was made, based on a Super Bowl commercial, to honor First Sergeants. It stated: "On the eighth day, God looked down on His creation and said, 'I need someone who will take care of the Airmen.' So God created a First Sergeant." Because the video mentioned the word "God," the Air Force required that it be taken down. [34]

June 2013 – An Army Master Sergeant is reprimanded, threatened with judicial action, and given a bad efficiency report, being told he was "no longer a team player," because he voiced his support of traditional marriage at his own promotion party. [35]

May 2013 - The Pentagon announces that "Air Force members are free to express their personal religious beliefs as long as it does not make others uncomfortable. "Proselytizing (inducing someone to convert to one's faith) goes over that line," [36] affirming if a sharing of faith makes someone feel uncomfortable that it could be a court-marital offense [37] -- the military equivalent of a civil felony.

May 2013 - An Air Force officer was actually made to remove a personal Bible from his own desk because it "might" appear that he was condoning the particular religion to which he belonged. [38]

April 2013 – Officials briefing U.S. Army soldiers placed "Evangelical Christianity" and "Catholicism" in a list that also included Al-Qaeda, Muslim Brotherhood, and Hamas as examples of "religious extremism." [39]

April 2013 – The U.S. Army directs troops to scratch off and paint over tiny Scripture verse references that for decades had been forged into weapon scopes. [40]

April 2013 - The Air Force creates a "religious tolerance" policy but consults only a militant atheist group to do so -- a group whose leader has described military personnel who are religious as 'spiritual rapists' and 'human monsters' [41] and who also says that soldiers who proselytize are guilty of treason and sedition and should be punished to hold back a "tidal wave of fundamentalists." [42]

January 2013 – President Obama announced his opposition to a provision in the 2013 National Defense Authorization Act protecting the rights of conscience for military chaplains. [43]

June 2012 – Bibles for the American military have been printed in every conflict since the American Revolution, but the Obama Administration revokes the long-standing U. S. policy of allowing military service emblems to be placed on those military Bibles. [44]

May 2012 – The Obama administration opposed legislation to protect the rights of conscience for military chaplains who do not wish to perform same-sex marriages in violation of their strongly-held religious beliefs. [45]

April 2012 – A checklist for Air Force Inns will no longer include ensuring that a Bible is available in rooms for those who want to use them. [46]

February 2012 – The U. S. Military Academy at West Point disinvites three star Army general and decorated war hero Lieutenant General William G. ("Jerry") Boykin (retired) from speaking at an event because he is an outspoken Christian. [47]

February 2012 – The Air Force removes "God" from the patch of Rapid Capabilities Office (the word on the patch was in Latin: Dei). [48]

February 2012 – The Army ordered Catholic chaplains not to read a letter to parishioners that their archbishop asked them to read. [49]

November 2011 – The Air Force Academy rescinds support for

Operation Christmas Child, a program to send holiday gifts to impoverished children across the world, because the program is run by a Christian charity. [50]

November 2011 – President Obama opposes inclusion of President Franklin Roosevelt's famous D-Day Prayer in the WWII Memorial. [51]

November 2011 – Even while restricting and disapprobating Christian religious expressions, the Air Force Academy pays $80,000 to add a Stonehenge-like worship center for pagans, druids, witches and Wiccans at the Air Force Academy. [52]

September 2011 – Air Force Chief of Staff prohibits commanders from notifying airmen of programs and services available to them from chaplains. [53]

September 2011 – The Army issues guidelines for Walter Reed Medical Center stipulating that "No religious items (i.e. Bibles, reading materials and/or facts) are allowed to be given away or used during a visit." [54]

August 2011 – The Air Force stops teaching the Just War theory to officers in California because the course is taught by chaplains and is based on a philosophy introduced by St. Augustine in the third century AD – a theory long taught by civilized nations across the world (except now, America). [55]

June 2011 – The Department of Veterans Affairs forbids references to God and Jesus during burial ceremonies at Houston National Cemetery. [56]

January 2010 – Because of "concerns" raised by the Department of Defense, tiny Bible verse references that had appeared for decades on scopes and gunsights were removed. [57]

3. Acts of hostility toward Biblical values:

March 2014 - The Obama administration seeks funding for every type of sex-education -- except that which reflects traditional moral values. [58]

August 2013 - Non-profit charitable hospitals, especially faith-based ones, will face large fines or lose their tax-exempt status if they don't comply with new strangling paperwork requirements related to giving free treatment to poor clients who do not have Obamacare insurance coverage. [59] Ironically, the first hospital in America was founded as a charitable institution in 1751 by Benjamin Franklin, and its logo was the Good Samaritan, with Luke 10:35 inscribed below him: "Take care of him, and I will repay thee," being designed specifically to offer free medical care to the poor. [60] Benjamin Franklin's hospital would likely be fined unless he placed more resources and funds into paperwork rather than helping the poor under the new faith-hostile policy of the Obama administration.

August 2013 - USAID, a federal government agency, shut down a conference in South Korea the night before it was scheduled to take place because some of the presentations were not pro-abortion but instead presented information on abortion complications, including the problems of "preterm births, mental health issues, and maternal mortality" among women giving birth who had previous abortions. [61]

June 2013 – The Obama Administration finalizes requirements that under the Obamacare insurance program, employers must make available abortion-causing drugs, regardless of the religious conscience objections of many employers and even despite the directive of several federal courts to protect the religious conscience of employers. [62]

April 2013 – The United States Agency for Internal Development (USAID), an official foreign policy agency of the U.S. government, begins a program to train homosexual activists in various countries around the world to overturn traditional marriage and anti-sodomy laws, targeting first those countries with strong Catholic influences, including Ecuador, Honduras, and Guatemala. [63]

December 2012 – Despite having campaigned to recognize Jerusalem as Israel's capital, President Obama once again suspends the provisions of the Jerusalem Embassy Act of 1995 which requires the United States to recognize Jerusalem as the capital of Israel and to move the American Embassy there. [64]

July 2012 - The Pentagon, for the first time, allows service members to wear their uniforms while marching in a parade - specifically, a gay pride parade in San Diego. [65]

October 2011 – The Obama administration eliminates federal grants to the U.S. Conference of Catholic Bishops for their extensive programs that aid victims of human trafficking because the Catholic Church is anti-abortion. [66]

September 2011 – The Pentagon directs that military chaplains may perform same-sex marriages at military facilities in violation of the federal Defense of Marriage Act. [67]

July 2011 – Obama allows homosexuals to serve openly in the

military, reversing a policy originally instituted by George Washington in March 1778. [68]

March 2011 – The Obama administration refuses to investigate videos showing Planned Parenthood helping alleged sex traffickers get abortions for victimized underage girls. [69]

February 2011 – Obama directs the Justice Department to stop defending the federal Defense of Marriage Act. [70]

September 2010 – The Obama administration tells researchers to ignore a judge's decision striking down federal funding for embryonic stem cell research. [71]

August 2010 – The Obama administration Cuts funding for 176 abstinence education programs. [72]

July 2010 – The Obama administration uses federal funds in violation of federal law to get Kenya to change its constitution to include abortion. [73]

September 16, 2009 – The Obama administration appoints as EEOC Commissioner Chai Feldblum, who asserts that society should "not tolerate" any "private beliefs," including religious beliefs, if they may negatively affect homosexual "equality." [74]

July 2009 – The Obama administration illegally extends federal benefits to same-sex partners of Foreign Service and Executive Branch employees, in direction violation of the federal Defense of Marriage Act. [75]

May 2009 – The White House budget eliminates all funding for abstinence-only education and replaces it with "comprehensive" sexual education, repeatedly proven to increase teen pregnancies and abortions. [76] He continues the deletion in subsequent budgets. [77]

May 2009 – Obama officials assemble a terrorism dictionary calling pro-life advocates violent and charging that they use racism in their "criminal" activities. [78]

March 2009 – The Obama administration shut out pro-life groups from attending a White House-sponsored health care summit. [79]

March 2009 – Obama orders taxpayer funding of embryonic stem cell research. [80]

March 2009 – Obama gave $50 million for the UNFPA, the UN population agency that promotes abortion and works closely with Chinese population control officials who use forced abortions and involuntary sterilizations. [81]

January 2009 – Obama lifts restrictions on U.S. government funding for groups that provide abortion services or counseling abroad, forcing taxpayers to fund pro-abortion groups that either promote or perform abortions in other nations. [82]

January 2009 – President Obama's nominee for deputy secretary of state asserts that American taxpayers are required to pay for abortions and that limits on abortion funding are unconstitutional. [83]

4. Acts of preferentialism for Islam:

February 2012 – The Obama administration makes effulgent apologies for Korans being burned by the U. S. military, [84] but when Bibles were burned by the military, numerous reasons were offered why it was the right thing to do. [85]

October 2011 – Obama's Muslim advisers block Middle Eastern Christians' access to the White House. [86]

August 2010 – Obama speaks with great praise of Islam and condescendingly of Christianity. [87]

August 2010 – Obama went to great lengths to speak out on multiple occasions on behalf of building an Islamic mosque at Ground Zero, while at the same time he was silent about a Christian church being denied permission to rebuild at that location. [88]

April 2010 – Christian leader Franklin Graham is disinvited from the Pentagon's National Day of Prayer Event because of complaints from the Muslim community. [89]

April 2010 – The Obama administration requires rewriting of government documents and a change in administration vocabulary to remove terms that are deemed offensive to Muslims, including jihad, jihadists, terrorists, radical Islamic, etc. [90]

May 2009 – While Obama does not host any National Day of Prayer event at the White House, he does host White House Iftar dinners in honor of Ramadan. [91]

2010 – While every White House traditionally issues hundreds of official proclamations and statements on numerous occasions, this White House avoids traditional Biblical holidays and events but regularly recognizes major Muslim holidays, as evidenced by its 2010 statements on Ramadan, Eid-ul-Fitr, Hajj, and Eid-ul-Adha.

[92]

Many of these actions are literally unprecedented – this is the first time they have happened in four centuries of American history. The hostility of President Obama toward Biblical faith and values is without equal from any previous American president.

References:

[1] Todd Starnes, "No Christmas in White House Holiday Card," Fox News Radio, 2011; Todd Starnes, "White House "Holiday" Card Spotlights Dog, Not Christmas," Fox News Radio, 2012; "White House Christmas Decor Featuring Mao Zedong Comes Under Fire," Fox News, December 24, 2009.
[2] Todd Starnes, "DOJ Defunds At-Risk Youth Programs over "God" Reference," Townhall, June 25, 2013.
[3] Steven Ertelt, "Obama Admin's HHS Mandate Revision Likely Excludes Hobby Lobby," LifeNews.com, February 1, 2013; Dan Merica, "Obama proposal would let religious groups opt-out of contraception mandate," CNN, February 1, 2013.
[4] Sheryl Gay Stolberg, "Minister Backs Out of Speech at Inaugural," New York Times, January 10, 2013; Eric Marrapodi, "Giglio bows out of inauguration over sermon on gays," CNN, January 10, 2013.
[5] Audrey Hudson, "Obama administration religious service for student loan forgiveness," Human Events, February 15, 2012.
[6] Ted Olson, "Church Wins Firing Case at Supreme Court," Christianity Today, January 11, 2012.
[7] Hillary Rodham Clinton, "Remarks in Recognition of International Human Rights Day," U.S. Department of State, December 6, 2011.
[8] Todd Starns, "Obama Administration Opposes FDR Prayer at WWII Memorial," Fox News, November 4, 2011.

[9] Joel Siegel, "Obama Omits God From Thanksgiving Speech, Riles Critics," ABC News, November 25, 2011.

[10] Chuck Donovan, "HHS's New Health Guidelines Trample on Conscience," Heritage Foundation, August 2, 2011.

[11] Chris Johnson, "ENDA passage effort renewed with Senate introduction," Washington Blade, April 15, 2011.

[12] Marrianne Medlin, "Amid criticism, President Obama moves to fill vacant religious ambassador post," Catholic News Agency, February 9, 2011; Thomas F. Farr, "Undefender of the Faith," Foreign Policy, April 5, 2012.

[13] LadyImpactOhio, " Feds sued by Veterans to allow stolen Mojave Desert Cross to be rebuilt," Red State, January 14, 2011.

[14] "Remarks by the President at the University of Indonesia in Jakarta, Indonesia," The White House, November 10, 2010.

[15] Meredith Jessup, "Obama Continues to Omit 'Creator' From Declaration of Independence," The Blaze, October 19, 2010.

[16] Johanna Neuman, "Obama end Bush-era National Prayer Day Service at White House," Los Angeles Times, May 7, 2009.

[17] Jim Lovino, "Jesus Missing From Obama's Georgetown Speech," NBC Washington, April 17, 2009.

[18] Chris McGreal, "Vatican vetoes Barack Obama's nominees for U.S. Ambassador," The Guardian, April 14, 2009.

[19] Aliza Marcus, "Obama to Lift 'Conscience' Rule for Health Workers," Bloomberg, February 27, 2009; Sarah Pulliam Baily, "Obama Admin. Changes Bush 'Conscience' Rule for Health Workers," Christianity Today, February 18, 2011.

[20] Sarah Pulliam Baily, "Obama: 'They cling to guns or religion'," Christianity Today, April 13, 2008.

[21] "Nativity scenes removed from Guantanamo dining halls after complaints," Fox News, December 19, 2013.

[22] Todd Starnes, "Nativity scenes removed from Guantanamo dining halls after complaints," Fox News, December 9, 2013.

[23] Steven Ertelt, "Army Briefing Tells Soldiers Christians and

Pro-Lifers are a "Radical" Threat," LifeNews, October 23, 2013.
[24] Todd Starnes, "Catholic priests in military face arrest for celebrating Mass," Fox News, October 5, 2013; The Brody File, "Priest: Obama Admin. Denied Mass to Catholics," CBN News, October 8, 2013.
[25] Stephen Losey, "Academy makes 'God' optional in cadets' oath," Air Force Times, October 25, 2013.
[26] Adan Salazar, "DoD Training Manual: 'Extremist' Founding Fathers 'Would Not Be Welcome In Today's Military'," infowars.com, August 24, 2013.
[27] Chad Groening, "'I cannot answer your question:' Air Force Sgt. says lesbian commander booted him," One News Now, August 20, 2013.
[28] "Military gives bonuses only to same-sex couples," WND, August 20, 2013.
[29] Melanie Korb, "Air Force Invites Drag Queens to Perform on 'Diversity Day'," Charisma News, August 19, 2013.
[30] Chad Groening, "Attorney demands answers for Air National Guard sergeant punished for beliefs," OneNewsNow, July 15, 2013.
[31] Todd Starnes, "Chaplain Ordered to Remove Religious Essay From Military Website," FoxNews Radio, July 24, 2013.
[32] Hellen Cook, "Pentagon Censors Christian Art," Christian News Wire, January 21, 2010.
[33] Todd Starnes, "Obama 'Strongly Objects' to Religious Liberty Amendment," Townhall, June 12, 2013.
[34] Todd Starnes, "Air Force Removes Video that Mentions God," Fox News Radio. June 7, 2013.
[35] Todd Starnes, "Army Punishes Soldier who Served Chick-fil-A," Fox News Radio, June 5, 2013.
[36] "Liberty Institute Calls On U.S. Department Of Defense To Abandon Shift In Military's Proselytizing Policy," PR Newswire, May 7, 2013; Todd Starnes, "Air Force Officer Told to Remove

Bible from Desk," Townhall.com, May 3, 2013.
[37] "Pentagon May Court Martial Soldiers Who Share Christian Faith," Breitbart, May 1, 2013.
[38] Todd Starnes, "Air Force Officer Told to Remove Bible from Desk," Townhall.com, May 3, 2013.
[39] Jack Minor, "Military Warned 'evangelicals' No. 1 Threat," WND, April 5, 2013.
[40] Todd Starnes, "Army Removes Bible Reference from Scopes," Fox News Radio, April 22, 2013.
[41] "Chaplain endorsers ask Air Force for equal time," Alliance Defending Freedom, April 30, 2013.
[42] Todd Starnes, "Pentagon: Religious Proselytizing is Not Permitted," Fox News Radio, April 30, 2013.
[43] Billy Hallowell, "Obama Opposes NDAA's 'Rights of Conscience' for Military Chaplains & Members, Vows to Protects Rights of Gays," The Blaze, January 4, 2013; Paul Conner, "Obama calls NDAA conscience clause for military chaplains 'unnecessary and ill-advised'," The Daily Caller, January 3, 2013.
[44] "Military Logos No Longer Allowed on Troop Bibles," CBN News, June 14, 2012.
[45] Patrick Goodenough, "White House 'Strongly Objects' to Legislation Protecting Military Chaplains from Doing Same-Sex Weddings or Being Forced to Act Against Conscience," cnsnews.com, May 16, 2012.
[46] Markeshia Ricks, "Bible checklist for Air Force lodges going away," Air Force Times, April 16, 2012.
[47] Ken Blackwell, "Gen. Boykin Blocked At West Point," cnsnews.com, February 1, 2012.
[48] Geoff Herbert, " Air Force unit removes 'God' from logo; lawmakers warn of 'dangerous precedent'," syracuse.com, February 9, 2012.
[49] Todd Starnes, "Army Silences Catholic Chaplains," Fox News Radio, February 6, 2012.

[50] "Air Force Academy Backs Away from Christmas Charity," Fox News Radio, November 4, 2011.

[51] Todd Starnes, "Obama Administration Opposes FDR Prayer at WWII Memorial," Fox News, November 4, 2011.

[52] Jenny Dean, "Air Force Academy adapts to pagans, druids, witches and Wiccans," Los Angeles Times, November 26, 2011.

[53] "Maintaining Government Neutrality Regarding Religion," Department of the Air Force, September 1, 2011.

[54] "Wounded, Ill, and Injured Partners in Care Guidelines," Department of the Navy (accessed on February 29, 2012).

[55] Jason Ukman, "Air Force suspends ethics course that used Bible passages that train missle launch officers," Washington Post, August 2, 2011.

[56] "Houston Veterans Claim Censorship of Prayers, Including Ban of 'God' and 'Jesus'," Fox News, June 29, 2011.

[57] Todd Spangler, "U.S. firm to remove Bible references from gun sights," USA Today, January 21, 2010.

[58] Steven Ertelt, "President Obama's Budget Eliminates Abstinence Education Programs," Life News, March 5, 2014; Jennifer Liberto, "Sex abstinence program among Obama's targeted cuts," CNN Money, March 5, 2014.

[59] Patrick Howley, "Obamacare installs new scrutiny, fines for charitable hospitals that treat uninsured people," The Daily Caller, August 8, 2013.

[60] "The Story of the Creation of the Nation's First Hospital," University of Pennsylvania Health System (accessed August 14, 2013).

[61] Wendy Wright," USAID Rep Shuts Down Workshop on Abortion Complications," Catholic Family & Human Rights Institute, August 9, 2013.

[62] "Obama Administration Ignores Outcries, Finalizes HHS Mandate Targeting Religious Freedom," Liberty Counsel, July 1, 2013; Baptist Press, "Moore, others: Final mandate rules fail,"

Townhall, July 1, 2013.
[63] Tony Perkins, "Obama administration begins training homosexual activists around the world," LifeSiteNews, June 6, 2013.
[64] Ken Blackwell, "Guest Opinion: Take a Risk for Peace. Move our Embassy to Jerusalem!," Catholic Online, June 5, 2013.
[65] "Pentagon: Service members now allowed to wear uniforms in gay pride parades," NY Daily News, July 19, 2012.
[66] Jerry Markon, "Health, abortion issues split Obama administration and Catholic groups," Washington Post, October 31, 2011.
[67] Luis Martinez, "Will Same Sex Marriages Pose a Dilemma for Military Chaplains?," ABC News, October 12, 2011.
[68] Elisabeth Bumiller, "Obama Ends 'Don't Ask, Don't Tell' Policy," New York Times, July 22, 2011; George Washington, The Writings of George Washington, John C. Fitzpatrick, editor (Washington: U. S. Government Printing Office, 1934), Vol. XI, pp. 83-84, from General Orders at Valley Forge on March 14, 1778.
[69] Steven Ertelt, "Obama Admin Ignores Planned Parenthood Sex Trafficking Videos," LifeNews, March 2, 2011.
[70] Brian Montopoli, "Obama administration will no longer defend DOMA," CBSNews, February 23, 2011.
[71] Steven Ertelt, "President Barack Obama's Pro-Abortion Record: A Pro-Life Compilation," LifeNews, February 11, 2012.
[72] Steven Ertelt, "Obama, Congress Cut Funding for 176 Abstinence Programs Despite New Study," LifeNews, August 26, 2010.
[73] Tess Civantos, "White House Spent $23M of Taxpayer Money to Back Kenyan Constitution That Legalizes Abortion, GOP Reps Say," Fox News, July 22, 2010.
[74] Matt Cover, "Obama's EEOC Nominee: Society Should 'Not Tolerate Private Beliefs' That 'Adversely Affect' Homosexuals,"

cnsnews.com, January 18, 2010.
[75] "Memorandum for the Heads of Executive Departments and Agencies," The White House, June 17, 2009.
[76] Steven Ertelt, "Barack Obama's Federal Budget Eliminates Funding for Abstinence-Only Education," LifeNews, May 8, 2009.
[77] Steven Ertelt, "Obama Budget Funds Sex Ed Over Abstinence on 16-1 Margin," LifeNews, February 14, 2011.
[78] Steven Ertelt, "Obama Admin Terrorism Dictionary Calls Pro-Life Advocates Violent, Racist," LifeNews, May 5, 2009.
[79] Steven Ertelt, "Pro-Life Groups Left Off Obama's Health Care Summit List, Abortion Advocates OK," LifeNews, March 5, 2009.
[80] "Obama Signs Order Lifting Restrictions on Stem Cell Research Funding," Fox News, March 9, 2009.
[81] Steven Ertelt, " Obama Administration Announces $50 Million for Pro-Forced Abortion UNFPA," LifeNews, March 26, 2009; Steven Ertelt, "President Barack Obama's Pro-Abortion Record: A Pro-Life Compilation," LifeNews, February 11, 2012.
[82] Jeff Mason and Deborah Charles, " Obama lifts restrictions on abortion funding," Reuters, January 23, 2009.
[83] "Obama pick: Taxpayers must fund abortions," World Net Daily, January 27, 2009.
[84] Masoud Popalzai and Nick Paton Walsh, " Obama apologizes to Afghanistan for Quran burning," CNN, February 23, 2012.
[85] "Military burns unsolicited Bibles sent to Afghanistan," CNN, May 22, 2009.
[86] "Report: Obama's Muslim Advisers Block Middle Eastern Christians' Access to the White House," Big Peace (accessed on February 29, 2012).
[87] Chuck Norris, " President Obama: Muslim Missionary? (Part 2)," Townhall.com, August 24, 2010; Chuck Norris, "President Obama: Muslim Missionary?," Townhall.com, August 17, 2010.
[88] Barack Obama, "Remarks by the President at Iftar Dinner,"

The White House, August 13, 2010; "Obama Comes Out in Favor of Allowing Mosque Near Ground Zero," Fox News, August 13, 2010; Pamela Geller, "Islamic Supremacism Trumps Christianity at Ground Zero," American Thinker, July 21, 2011.
[89] "Franklin Graham Regrets Army's Decision to Rescind Invite to Pentagon Prayer Service," Fox News, April 22, 2010.
[90] "Obama Bans Islam, Jihad From National Security Strategy Document," Fox News, April 7, 2010; "Counterterror Adviser Defends Jihad as 'Legitimate Tenet of Islam'," Fox News, May 27, 2010; "'Islamic Radicalism' Nixed From Obama Document," CBSNews, April 7, 2010.
[91] Barack Obama, " Remarks by the President at Iftar Dinner," The White House, September 1, 2009; Kristi Keck, " Obama tones down National Day of Prayer observance," CNN, May 6, 2009; Dan Gilgoff, "The White House on National Day of Prayer: A Proclamation, but No Formal Ceremony," U.S. News, May 1, 2009.
[92] "WH Fails to Release Easter Proclamation," Fox Nation, April 25, 2011; "President Obama ignores most holy Christian holiday; AFA calls act intentional," American Family Association (accessed on February 29, 2012).

This article above was published by WallBuilders, LLC, a Texas Limited Liability Corporation. They may be contacted at PO Box 397, Aledo, Texas, 76008.

Insert

The names 'Antichrist' and 'Beast' are somewhat confusing. Some believe the two are one and the same. That's possible. Perhaps those words were used interchangeably in most of the Bible, but not necessarily. The irony is that most references made about the antichrist are to the Book of Revelation, speaking of the beast and 666 concepts. In fact, the word or the description as the antichrist does not appear in Revelation. The word beast appears many times.

The concept of 'beast' and 'antichrist' could be separate and different except for one critical criteria. The antichrists claim to be Jesus, or they allow themselves to be considered Jesus. This special one, the beast, also allows himself to be considered Jesus, the Messiah, and eventually sits in the place of God in Jerusalem. When will the beast appear? It seems the 'old dragon' will make that determination. Satan will choose the beast when he thinks the time is right. This is indicated by Revelation 13:1-2:

> "And I stood upon the sand of the sea, and saw a beast rise up out of the sea, having seven heads and ten horns, and upon his horns ten crowns, and upon his heads the name of blasphemy.

> 2 And the beast which I saw was like unto a leopard, and his feet were as the feet of a bear, and his mouth as the mouth of a lion: and the dragon gave him his power, and his seat, and great authority."

Continued on page 100

Chapter 5

Why the Hatred for Christianity

From the 'Jeremiah Project': Jesus warned his disciples and explained why there exists a hatred for Christianity.

"If the world hates you, keep in mind that it hated me first. If you belonged to the world, it would love you as its own. As it is, you do not belong to the world, but I have chosen you out of the world. That is why the world hates you.

Remember the words I spoke to you: 'No servant is greater than his master.' If they persecuted me, they will persecute you also. If they obeyed my teaching, they will obey yours also. They will treat you this way because of my name, for they do not know the One who sent me. If I had not come and spoken to them, they would not be guilty of sin. Now, however, they have no excuse for their sin. He who hates me hates my Father as well. If I had not done among them what no one else did, they would not be guilty of sin. But now they have seen these miracles, and yet they have hated both me and my Father. But this is to fulfill what is written in their Law: 'They hated me without reason.'" - John 15:18-25

What Christians are experiencing in the world today is not so much a "war on Christianity" as it is rebellion against God, and thus a hatred toward anything that points to God or His Son Jesus... and by extension a hatred of Christ's followers.

In recent decades, we have seen worldwide an escalating of this hatred of Christianity in the form of militant radical Islam. While this Islamic jihad has been exploding for years throughout the Middle East and Europe, it burst on the scene in America on September 11, 2001.

Many Islamic-dominated nations have adopted a fanatical, militant doctrine of persecution against all "infidels."

Close U.S. ally, Saudi Arabia has no religious freedom, all citizens must adhere to Sunni Islam. Others are imprisoned, tortured, detained, etc. for engaging in other religious activities. Apostasy is punishable by death. There are no public worship services for non-Muslims. Anyone who does mission work or converts Muslims faces expulsion, jail, or execution.

Since the September 11, 2001 attacks on the United States where 15 of the 19 hijackers were citizens of Saudi Arabia, the Saudi government has failed to implement a number of promised reforms related to promoting freedom of thought, conscience, and religion or belief. The Saudi government persists in banning all forms of public religious expression other than that of the government's own interpretation of one school of Sunni Islam; prohibits churches, synagogues, temples, and other non-Muslim places of worship; uses in its schools and posts online state textbooks that continue to espouse intolerance and incite violence; and periodically interferes with private religious practice.

The militant Islamic Government of Sudan severely restricts religious practice of all other types of religion and their restrictive Shari'ah law

(Islamic law) attacks and threatens the Christian community. They are waging a self-described religious war against Christian, non-Muslim, and moderate Muslim persons by using torture, starvation, enslavement, and murder. They have violations of apostasy that could ultimately end up in the death penalty.

In Egypt (where the U.S. supported Arab Spring erupted that led to the overthrow of Hosni Mubarak), there continues to be serious problems of discrimination, intolerance, and other violations against religious minorities. Military and security forces are known to use excessive force and live ammunition targeting Coptic Christian demonstrators and places of worship resulting in dozens of deaths and hundreds of injuries. The government also continues to prosecute, convict, and imprison Egyptian citizens charged with blasphemy.

In U.S. occupied Afghanistan, the constitution and other laws and policies restrict religious freedom and, in practice the government generally enforced legal restrictions. Non-Muslim minority groups, particularly Christians, Hindus, and Sikhs, continue to be targets of persecution and discrimination. Shia and Sunni Islamic clergy, as well as many citizens, interpreted conversion from Islam as contravening the tenets of Islam. Conversion, considered an act of apostasy and a crime against Islam, could be punishable by death if the convert did not recant.

In Iraq, the government continues to tolerate systematic, ongoing, and egregious religious freedom violations. Religious sites and worshippers are targeted in violent attacks, often with impunity, and businesses viewed as "un - Islamic" are vandalized.

In Pakistan, the government has declared those that who "insult" Mohammed will be put to death. In Communist Laos more than 250 pastors and Christian workers have been arrested; more than 60 churches and Christian institutions have been shut down; and the government has forced many thousands of believers to sign documents to "renounce" their faith and belief in Christianity.

Other offenders of religious freedom according to the United States Commission on International Religious Freedom also include Burma, China, Egypt, Eritrea, Iran, Nigeria, North Korea, Pakistan, Tajikistan, Turkey, Turkmenistan, Uzbekistan, and Vietnam. The CPC watch list of countries considered borderline and many eventually end up with aggressive religious persecution include: Belarus, Cuba, India, Indonesia, Laos, Russia, Somalia, and Venezuela.

In more than 40 nations around the world, people are being persecuted simply because of their faith. Hundreds of men and women are in prison serving sentences that range from a few months to life. They are not criminals who have robbed or murdered other citizens but Christians who were put on trial for their faith in Christ and found guilty. Christians are beaten, tortured, imprisoned, and murdered by those who are hostile to their faith in Jesus Christ.

The Third Jihad

The U.S. government trained, armed, funded and supported Osama bin Laden and his followers in Afghanistan. Zbigniew Brzezinski admitted that President Carter authorized the covert sponsorship of Muslim extremists, thus creating the mujahadeen and Al Qeada in Afghanistan in the 1980s to fight against Soviet aggression. In Afghanistan and then in Bosnia, the U.S. sponsored Muslim terror even as the State Department was officially condemning it.

In 2012, the Obama administration Secretary of State Hillary Rodham Clinton approved $1.3 billion in military aid in the form of F-16 fighter jets, M1 tanks, and similar weaponry to the Muslim Brotherhood in Egypt. Senator Rand Paul said, "I think it is a blunder of the first proportion to send sophisticated weapons to a country that allowed a mob to attack our embassy and to burn our flag. I find it objectionable to send weapons, F-16s and tanks to a country that allowed a mob chanting 'death to America' to threaten our American diplomats." Paul also stated that "these weapons threaten Israel's security" and "someday may be used against Israel."

The United States has also been supporting al Qeada affiliates in the Libyan civil war and Syrian civil war. While the Obama Administration has been very open about their support for the rebels, they apparently went to great lengths to cover up the arms shipments to al Qeada groups in Syria when it issued stand down orders to prevent the murders of four American citizens, including Ambassador Christopher Stevens in it's Benghazi consulate. The New York Times reported that since early 2012, the CIA has been aiding Arab governments and Turkey in obtaining and shipping weapons to the Syrian rebels. Days after the Benghazi attack that killed U.S. Ambassador Christopher Stevens, WND broke the story that Stevens himself played a central role in recruiting jihadists to fight Assad's regime in Syria, according to Egyptian and other Middle Eastern security officials.

During an interview with CNBC's Larry Kudlow, radio talk show host John Baxter said "Benghazi is not about Libya, Benghazi is about the policy of the Obama administration to involve the United States without clarity to the American people, not only in Libya but throughout the whole of the Arab world now in turmoil," Baxter told Kudlow. "Benghazi is about the NSC directing an operation that is perhaps shadowy, perhaps has a presidential finding, perhaps doesn't, that takes arms and men and puts them into Syria in the guise of the Free Syria Army."

Paul Mulshine of The Star Ledger asks, "Do you support the call by John McCain and Lindsey Graham for the U.S. to intervene on the side of the rebels in Syria? Congratulations! You're on the same side as the Muslim Brotherhood and Al Qaeda." The Muslim Brotherhood has been trying to overthrow the Assad regime since 1982 and joined with Al Qaeda to put together such operations as the Sept. 11 attack on New York. And now they're trying to take over Syria with the support of the United States.

Senator Rand Paul said of McCain's visit with Syrian rebels, "People say, 'Assad is such a bad guy.' He is. But on the other side we have alQaeda and now Nusra. So there's two ironies you have to overcome if you want to get involved in a war in Syria," he continued. "The first irony is you will be allied with al Qaeda. The second irony is most of the Christians are on the other side, so you may be arming Islamic rebels who may well be killing Christians. Does that make Assad a good person? No. I don't think there are any good people in this war, and there are some tragically innocent people who are going to be caught in the middle. But I just don't know that arming one side is going to make the tragedy any less."

Never before in American history have Christians experienced being hated for following Jesus Christ as they are today.

While the war on Christianity in America and persecution of Christians has not yet reached the feverish pitch of persecution as it has in other parts of the world, there is a battle being waged and the Antichrist forces are making progress. Executive orders have been signed by our President, labor camps have been setup, our government has stockpiled guns and ammo, and Christians have been put on the terrorist list. It would seem we are getting close to the day that here in American we will suffer extreme persecution.

Currently, there is still a Constitution in America that protects Christians and allows them to freely practice their faith. But, broiling beneath the surface, the same hatred of God that exists in other parts of the world is festering in all our institutions. Slowly, methodically, and incrementally the anti-God forces are working to remove that Constitutional barrier and replace it with the 10 Planks of Communism.

Forces within our government even use the so-called "war on terror" as a mechanism to actually support the enemies of our freedom. Following the 9/11 attacks, the U.S. Government has instituted numerous laws and regulations that strip Americans of the Constitutional rights and in some cases even paint Bible believing Christians as terrorists.

"But know this, that in the last days perilous times will come: For men will be lovers of themselves, lovers of money, boasters, proud, blasphemers, disobedient to parents, unthankful, unholy, unloving, unforgiving, slanderers, without self-control, brutal, despisers of good, traitors, headstrong, haughty, lovers of pleasure rather than lovers of God…. And from such people turn away!

…all who desire to live godly in Christ Jesus will suffer persecution. But evil men and impostors will grow worse and worse, deceiving and being deceived. But you must continue in the things which you have learned …" 2 Timothy 3:1-5, 12-14

It is important to recognize that those engaged in the war on Christianity, working for the dissolution of our society and breakdown of the family have a spiritual agenda. They are not merely attempting to dismantle the historic cultural values of this nation and move us toward a new world order. They also want to destroy Christianity and Bible-based religion. It is a clear part of their agenda, and they have already moved a long way in that direction.

"Then you will be handed over to be persecuted and put to death, and you will be hated by all nations because of me." - Matt. 24:9

It was prophesied 2,000 years ago that Christians will be hated and ultimately handed over to be persecuted and put to death. The fulfillment of this prophecy began soon after Christ said it. Stephen was stoned (Acts 7:59); James was killed by Herod (Acts 12:2); and, the persecution under Nero took place before the destruction of Jerusalem, in which were put to death, with many others, Peter and Paul. Most of the apostles, it is believed, died by persecution. This prophecy was fulfilled then, and has been in all ages since.

Modernday Christians continue to witness the fulfillment of this prophecy even today. God hating zealots include people like David Rockefeller, Henry Kissinger, Zbigniew Brzezinsky, and the other politicos, European Royalty, world bankers and CEO's of multinational corporations who are members of the Council on Foreign Relations, the Bilderberg group and the Trilateral Commission. Their stated plan is to have a one world government which is opposed to God and Christ.

Our entertainment industry and the news media sneer at anyone who defends Jesus Christ in public and have been leading a propaganda war of stereotyping Christians into a subordinate class. Their distortions reflect a genuine misunderstanding of who Christians are and what they believe.

Americas' mainstream news media ignores conservative and Christian news events, except when coverage makes religious leaders look "cold, intolerant and oppressive," says Washington, D.C.'s Media Research Center. Their coverage of the anti-Christian agenda is all but ignored and rarely reported on. Of course, that is understandable when you realize they are part of the anti-christian cabal and have agreed not to cover what is discussed at the globalist meetings they attend .

Though most Americans believe in God and regularly attend religious services, "religion and religious issues are hardly ever mentioned, much less covered, on network television morning, evening and magazine shows," said the center's chairman Brent Bozell. He said that the center has surveyed more than 18,000 nightly news shows broadcast by ABC, CBS, NBC, the Cable News Network and the Public Broadcasting Service, but found only 212 stories that focused on religion. That amounts to 1 percent of coverage although 52 percent of Americans say they attend church and more than 90 percent say that they pray regularly.

Network coverage of abortion and homosexuality "are never done from the religious viewpoint," Bozell said. Instead, "religious figures are regularly portrayed as reactionary roadblocks while their positive influences are rarely covered." Except at Christmastime, when the networks traditionally broadcast "heartwarming" segments in their broadcasts, the news shows usually portray religious groups and their leaders "as cold, intolerant and oppressive," Bozell said. ["TV news broadcasters unfair to Christians, says research center," Christian Crusade, April 1994]

Government

The federal government abridges the free exercise of religion in America by:

1. Regulating churches and other religious organizations through its tax laws. In 2013, the IRS admitted to targeting conservative and Christian groups for greater scrutiny.

Among the organizations the IRS investigated and audited were the Billy Graham Evangelistic Association (BGEA) and the 180-year-old Baptist newspaper the Biblical Recorder, published by the North Carolina Baptist State Convention. The IRS reportedly also targeted the humanitarian relief group Samaritan's Purse. Both it and the

BGEA are run by Franklin Graham, son of famed evangelical preacher Billy Graham.

The Washington Examiner reported that the IRS refused to approve an application of tax exempt status for a group called the Coalition for Life of Iowa unless it sent a letter certifying that it would not picket against Planned Parenthood. In addition, the Coalition was asked by the IRS about the content of its prayers.

The Weekly Standard reported that Lois Lerner, director of the IRS's Exempt Organizations Division, was accused of politically motivated harassment after a huge investigation into the Christian Coalition in the 1990s.

2. Limiting religious liberty in the area of public and private education.

3. Forbidding non-denominational prayer in public schools and at educational ceremonies.

4. Excluding the Bible from school classrooms and from other school property.

5. Refusing to permit the religious displays on public property, such as Christmas and Chanukah.

Navy Lt. Gordon James Klingenschmitt was punished by a commander for offering sectarian prayers at a memorial service for a fallen sailor.

Schools

Possibly the most sinister battlefield in the war on Christianity takes place in the classroom. The Ten Commandments have been prohibited on school bulletin boards and most forms of prayer have been declared unconstitutional in the nation's schools, even that which is student initiated.

Atheists and others who hate God despise Christians who help others come to a saving knowledge of Christ. They are determined to battle those who would help immature Christians -- particularly Christian children -- grow in their relationship with Jesus Christ.

Increasingly, our children are discriminated against for trying to present their Christian convictions in school.

In 1997 U.S. District Court Judge Ira DeMent struck down a law that required schools to allow voluntary student-initiated prayers at school events, saying it created excessive state entanglement in religion. He ordered the end to school-sponsored religious activities, such as prayers during morning announcements and at school events even though it isn't forced on students.

A high school student in Florida was suspended for handing out religious literature before and after - but not during - school hours. Two high school students in Texas were told by their principal they could not wear rosaries. The Principal claimed that they were symbols of gang activity, even though the boys were not involved in any gang.

In 2002, music teachers in Michigan, Maryland, and Virginia didn't allow students to perform traditional carols like "Silent Night" and "The First Noel" during Christmas. A New Jersey public school banned the Charles Dickens play, "A Christmas Carol" because of its spiritual overtones and message of redemption.

Writing for the majority in U.S. v. Windsor (which declared the Defense of Marriage Act (DOMA) unconstitutional), Supreme Court Justice Anthony Kennedy wrote a anti-christian polemic disguised as a legal opinion attacking the Christian concept of marriage saying that those who stand up for traditional marriage, i.e. Christians, has an animus against gays, want to deny them equal dignity, want to brand them as unworthy, and has a hateful desire to harm a politically unpopular group. This God hating, pagan judge essentially branded Christians as a hate group, opening the door for future oppression by the courts. Apparently, Justice Kennedy perceives himself or at least the Court to be God with supremacy over the people in violation of the religious freedom and liberty guaranteed by the Constitution.

Declaration of Independence

Our rights come from God, not government. Our Founders enshrined that notion in the Declaration of Independence saying, "We hold these truths to be self-evident, that all men are created equal, that they are endowed by their Creator with certain unalienable Rights, that among these are Life, Liberty and the pursuit of Happiness." Justice Kennedy is NOT the law giver God and the other justices are not on the bench to take away those rights "endowed by their Creator" while granting new laws and rights not envisioned by the Founders or the American people. In fact, the purpose of government, including the Judicial Branch, are addressed in the next sentence of the Declaration, "That to secure these rights, Governments are instituted among Men, deriving their just powers from the consent of the governed." We the people "consent" to the powers of Justice Kennedy and others to "secure these rights," not take them away.

Perhaps it's time We the People withdraw our consent from those working to dissolve our Constitution and failing to secure the rights given us by God. Not coincidentally, the Declaration also addresses that issue in it's next sentence, "That whenever any Form of Government becomes destructive of these ends, it is the Right of the People to alter or to abolish it, and to institute new Government, laying its foundation on such principles and organizing its powers in such form, as to them shall seem most likely to effect their Safety and Happiness."

Judge Roy Moore in Gadsden, Alabama, was ordered to stop conducting prayers in his courtroom and displaying the Ten Commandments. That led Alabama Gov. Fob James, a supporter of prayer in public schools, to vow to use state troopers, if necessary, to allow Moore to continue the prayers.

Confessed child rapist James Arnett's sentence was overturned by an Ohio appeals court. The reason: the judge in his case quoted from Matthew 18:5-6 during sentencing.

The Public Square

The secularist trend in the public forum is to replace the word "Christmas" with "Season's Greetings" or "Happy Holidays."

In March 1998, The ACLU put pressure on the small town of Republic, Missouri to remove a fish symbol from its official logo, calling it a "secret sign of Christianity."

In April 1998, Rev. Patrick Mahoney was arrested for praying on the steps of the Supreme Court.

Tourists visiting Washington D.C. in 1997 were ordered by the police to stop praying in the rotunda of the U.S. Capitol.

In 2003, the National Park Service removed 30 year-old plaques inscribed with Bible verses at Grand Canyon following complaints from the American Civil Liberties Union.

The Workplace

The anti-Christian bias is a reality in many companies today -- as you will discover if you refuse to work on Sundays, if you question "shading the truth" in presentations, or if you stubbornly hold to your Christian standards.

A Christian employee of Hewlet Packard was fired for posting Bible verses condemning homosexual behavior on his desk in response to posters displayed during a company campaign to promote a diverse work force. (WorldNetDaily)

Businesses

Even though Krispy Kreme promises to give students a free doughnut for each "A" on their report cards, a store in Schereville, Indiana refused to reward the Kamp children for A's received in Bible classes. ["Chain Won't Give a Doughnut for an 'A' in Bible", Wendy Cloyd, Assistant Editor, CitizenLink]

David and Barbara Green, the devout Christian Hobby Lobby owners, David and Barbara Green, only want to live the American dream and to be free to do business according to their beliefs. They seek to honor God in their business by "operating their company in a manner consistent with Biblical principles."

But, HHS secretary Kathleen Sebelius and the Obama administration thinks otherwise. The Oklahoma-based Hobby Lobby company sued the Obama administration in September 2012 regarding the U.S. Department of Health and Human Services' abortion-pill mandate, a regulation under the Affordable Care Act (aka Obamacare), requiring the chains to offer potential abortion-inducing drugs in their employee health-care plans.

The U.S. Supreme Court announced in Nov. 2013, it will take up Sebelius v. Hobby Lobby Stores, Inc. case addressing the

Constitutionally guaranteed rights of business owners to operate their family companies without violating their deeply held religious convictions.

This case has ramifications far beyond abortifacients such as the morning after pill. The pagan mandates in Obamacare also include sterilizations and sex change operations. If this law is allowed to stand, the legal precedent will be set for these kind of immoral practices to explode along with other even more evil practices.

Steve Deace said on his radio program there is a danger here with the Supreme Court hearing this case. If the Court says the Christians at Hobby Lobby do not have to do what their pagan government told them to do because they have a First Amendment right to object, then you have all kinds of rights to object to being compelled to participate in all kinds of immorality that the government wants you to accept. If the Court rules for Hobby Lobby here, it will severely undercut it's own landmark ruling in the DOMA case. Given the Court's recent history, I wouldn't expect them to defend Christian religious freedom.

Michael Peroutka of the Institute on the Constitution points out that the centralized government is exerting itself to be God and to force it's brand of morality on the people rather than seeing itself as the agent supposed to protect those rights given by God and guaranteed by the Constitution.

Christians Standing United

"All men will hate you because of me, but he who stands firm to the end will be saved." - Matt. 10:22

Like-minded Christians should be standing firm together in our struggles while supporting and loving one another (John 15:17; Rom. 12:9-13). Instead of cooperating with unbelievers, we should "shake the dust off your feet when you leave that home or town." (Matt. 10:14) We should refuse any further connection with them.

"You adulterous people, don't you know that friendship with the world is hatred toward God? Anyone who chooses to be a friend of the world becomes an enemy of God." - James 4:4

Turn OFF that ungodly television, stop going to their theaters, defy the governments unjust laws, stand in contempt in their corrupt courtrooms, stop voting for their corrupt politicians and demand government to return to just weights and measures, remove your children from their secular humanist public schools, fire your MD and stop using those drug pushers to attend to your health, free yourself from the slavery of employment if you're working for an ungodly company, boycott the products of ungodly businesses and multi-national corporations and instead support those products and services of fellow believers. Read A Christian Patriot Action Plan to Resist the New World Order for a more complete manifesto of patriotic Christian activism. And, instead of being intimidated in the public square, Christians should be flooding that arena with the message, "The kingdom of heaven is near." (Matt. 10:7)

"Do not conform any longer to the pattern of this world, but be transformed by the renewing of your mind." - Romans 12:2

"5 We know that the earthly tent we live in will be destroyed. But we have a building made by God. It is a house in heaven that lasts forever. Human hands did not build it.

2 During our time on earth we groan. We long to put on our house in heaven as if it were clothing. 3 Then we will not be naked.

4 While we live in this tent of ours, we groan under our heavy load. We don't want to be naked. We want to be dressed with our house in

heaven. What must die will be swallowed up by life.

5 God has made us for that very purpose. He has given us the Holy Spirit as a down payment. The Spirit makes us sure of what is still to come.

6 So here is what we can always be certain about. As long as we are at home in our bodies, we are away from the Lord. 7 We live by believing, not by seeing. 8 We are certain about that. We would rather be away from our bodies and at home with the Lord. 9 So we try our best to please him. We want to please him whether we are at home in our bodies or away from them.

10 We must all stand in front of Christ to be judged. Each one of us will be judged for the good things and the bad things we do while we are in our bodies. Then each of us will receive what we are supposed to get."

Instead of conforming to this world, true Christians are called to be different. Christians should be doing everything possible to get off the world's grid. In addition to the things above a Christian can do, I would also suggest a renewal of your mind from the godless propaganda that has distorted your beliefs of just about everything. Learn the truth about the people, places, and things that have been influencing your life and the Antichrist will ultimately use to deceive even the elect (Matt. 24:24). Wake Up!

"No man can serve two masters: for either he will hate the one, and love the other; or else he will hold to the one, and despise the other. Ye cannot serve God and mammon." - Matt. 6:24 (KJV)

I am not suggesting the above actions from a reconstructionist theology point of view. I certainly don't expect Christians are going to change the world into some heavenly utopia. You and I are not going to save the world. We can, however, influence some individuals and help them find the saving grace of God. And, I believe we are each individually responsible for our own choices of whom we serve. My prayer for you and I is that we come to the end of our time and hear, "Well done, good and faithful servant; thou hast been faithful over a few things, I will make thee ruler over many things: enter thou into the joy of thy lord." (Matt. 25:23, KJV) **End of the Jeremiah Project article.**

In reference 10 above it states, "while we are in our bodies." This comment brings into question about the soul - what is the soul that ascends to Heaven - or elsewhere? This is perhaps the greatest question of and about religion. This question regarding the existence of the 'soul' perhaps is the determining question for our purpose, our existence, and our destiny. Without a 'soul' would the question of religion even be applicable?

Without a soul our life of movement, energy, and thought would just cease - totally, and without a purpose for life to have been here in the first place. If that were the case, then this question of the three denials would have no purpose. Perhaps the idea of a 'soul' concerns belief. Revelation, Chapters 6 and 13 perhaps give a clue.

Chapter 6, Verse 9 begins: "And when he had opened the fifth seal, I saw under the alter the souls of them that were slain for the word of God, and for the testimony which they held: 10, And they cried with a loud voice saying, How long, O Lord, holy and true, dost thou not judge and avenge our blood on them that dwell on the earth? 11, ---- and it was said unto them, that they should rest yet for a little season, until their fellowservants also and their brethren, that should be killed as they were, should be fulfilled."

The 'others to be killed' is explained in Chapter 13. These killings, mentioned elsewhere as beheadings, take place after the second beast (the second antichrist) promotes an image of the first beast (the first antichrist) for everyone to worship. This will take place after the one world leader is appointed by Satan to become the 'beast.' The word 'antichrist' is not used in Revelation. This happens when the 'seven heads' rise from the sea and are joined - the seven continents having ten major kingdoms. If the antichrist exists today, he does not recognize that he will become, or is, the antichrist. He will be appointed by Satan at the designated time, after the '7 heads' are joined. Until then, the coming antichrist, and his many followers, will believe he is doing wonderful things for mankind.

Chapter 13, Verse 14: ----saying to them that dwell on the earth, that they should make an image to the beast, which had the wound by a sword, and did live. (Another chapter explains that the beast was attacked and had miraculously survived, giving the appearance he should be worshiped - therefore the image of worship.) Verse 15: And he had power to give life unto the image of the beast, that the image of the beast should both speak, and cause that as many as would not worship the image of the beast should be killed. Verse 16: And he causeth all, both small and great, rich and poor, free and bond, to receive a mark in their right hand, or in their foreheads. (When John wrote Revelation over 2000 years ago, he didn't know about computers and holograms that could speak. Today, this verse is more realistic and understandable.)

Now, continuing this increasingly unpopular dialogue about God, Christianity, religion, and a soul, the soul itself should be considered for the whole discussion to make any sense - to have any relativity. Before I begin this topic I must add that these religious topics are becoming more unacceptable to more people. It seems more people are rejecting God and the idea of Jesus Christ as His earthly representative.

Not many years ago, no one would have expressed such distaste or animosity against the idea of God. Several of my 24 published books mention God or discuss religious principles. The only negative reviews of my books are that some of the content of those books discuss religion. They vehemently express their disbelief in and rejection of God. And, this idea seems to be rapidly growing under the current Obama administration. This attack on God and Christianity, and the Jewish religion, demands a response. Many are afraid to speak or write boldly and openly about Christian principles. They know they will be criticized and condemned - as verses in the Bible prophesied - for the last days. Regardless, the concept of the 'soul' must be considered for Christianity to make any sense in a real world.

Of course, no mortal really knows what a soul is; and I certainly wouldn't suggest I know or understand. However, there are some modern ideas and discoveries that offer at least little tidbits of theory. Let's consider electricity, cells, and energy molecules we know are there but don't understand their sources.

So, what about electricity - or something comparable to or similar to electricity? We can't see electricity; does that mean it doesn't exist? What if God is not an old white-haired man often personified in art; what if God is not human-like at all? Does that mean He could not exist in form such as electricity? According to scripture, Jesus was sent in human form as God's visible representative. If electricity were connected throughout the universe, and it all led back to one central source, could that not create a divine connection between God and humanity? Would that source not last forever and ever?

We can also consider human cells. Human cells don't just hang around in our bodies as fat little blobs killing time. Each of the billions of them has a purpose, and they are given energy to fulfill their purpose. What if one of those cells, or invisible energy sources, hidden somewhere in our body was the 'life' cell, the one planted at conception to make the attachment to God and His universe. Do all cells and all energy have to die when one dies? Have you ever heard of spores? Some live forever. Is it inconceivable that a single cell could hold the hereafter energy until time for resurrection? Is it not possible that that small amount of space and energy could hold all our thoughts of the past and our expectations of the future back to our original source? Is it not possible that when the 'Book of Life' is opened for judgement, we are not there opening ourselves to judge ourselves?

Perhaps Heaven is that re-connection to the God source to live forever and ever. Perhaps Hell is the realization one judges himself or herself that he or she rejected that eternal connection during his or her lifetime, and therefore that self-judgement never got instilled into the 'forever' cell. Perhaps that invisible energy source flows through the universe forever with the lasting sense of not recognizing or respecting its original source. Perhaps Hell is nowhere and nonexistence and is the antithesis of awareness of belonging to the eternal life source. Perhaps. Perhaps only God knows.

Insert

The first verse in Chapter 13 says, "---saw a beast rise up out of the sea, having seven heads." Why is the number seven important?

Seven is considered 'God's' number. Many things, He numbered seven, including the days of the week. And, we can't forget the seven biblical churches, the seven vials of disaster, and the seven angels. Many things in the Bible and in nature have the number seven attached to them. The one most important to the identification of the beast, however, is the number seven - of the seven continents.

Is there anything other than the seven continents that rise up from the sea? This critical clue is that the beast will rise when the seven heads, the seven continents are united. (Other references to the 'sea' refer to the sea of mankind. This reference includes the 'sand' of the sea, which suggests it's not a reference to that 'mankind' sea.)

Verse 2 says that's when "the dragon gave him his power, and his seat, and great authority." Since this verse includes the seven continents and 'great authority' that can only mean one thing. The beast will be created when the world is under one leader. This is currently defined as 'The New World Order.' Another clue that supports this one-world concept is in Daniel 7:23, which says:

> "The fourth beast shall be the fourth kingdom upon earth, which shall be diverse from all kingdoms, and shall devour the whole earth, and shall tread it down, and break it to pieces."

Continued on page 118

100

Chapter 6

Related Articles

Iran

Why is Iran so determined to attack Israel? Of course, Muslims would like to recapture Jerusalem and, in doing so, wipe Israel off the face of the earth. And, why are many of Iran's Muslim neighbors not openly supporting Iran's aggression? There are two important reasons.

First, Iran has a long history of aggression and domination as the Persian Empire. If you recall, King Xerxes of Persia was the force that destroyed the Spartan 300 at the battle of Thermopole on his way to capture Athens. His father, King Cyrus, was just as vicious in his zeal to conquer and control his neighbors, especially Asia Minor, now Turkey.

It began with the Persians attacking Lydian King Croesus at Sardis, which had what was considered an impenetrable fortress. Sardis is one of the seven churches later referenced in the Book of Revelation. John referenced the 'beware the thief in the night' phrase to warn Christians to be alert to distractions. This reference is to a weakness the Persians found that allowed them to conquer that high impenetrable fortress. They watched a Lydian soldier go down a secret path to recover his lost helmet. In darkness, they invaded through that hidden path.

Secondly, Iran will not be deterred from creating havoc. In fact, the Imams in Iran seek havoc, chaos, and confusion in that part of the world. Their irresponsible actions have to do with their interpretation of what they consider their 'Mahdi,' also considered the 'Twelfth Imam.' It's their Messiah.

Iran is a mostly Shiite country, and along with Yemen are the two major Shiite locations. Shiites believe the Mahdi, their Messiah, is waiting on the sidelines for the world to get so chaotic that he will appear to make the world pure - pure Muslim. At the moment they consider him in 'occultation,' which means he is already on earth but hasn't shown himself - and will not until the world is turned upside down. He's just waiting for the right sign.

 The Sunnis also believe in the Mahdi, but they don't believe in the 'occultation' phase. According to them, the Mahdi has not arrived yet. This is the great rift that keeps the Muslims from acting as one, along with tribalism. This is very similar to the difference of belief in the Christian Messiah, versus the Jewish Messiah.

Anyway, don't expect the Iranians to back down to any pressure, or to become what we would consider rational. They are focused on making their Mahdi appear to reshape the world. My book, '666: Mark of the Beast,' refers further to these characters and concepts.

Obama's Ring: His Symbol of Evil

How did the serpent come to represent the devil, Satan, to be 'Satan's seat' in Pergamum, often pronounced Pergamos? It was established by an Attalus prince. During the Attalid dynasty from 214-133 B.C., in what is now the country of Turkey, Prince Archias went to the Temple of Aesculapius in Epidaurus, Greece to recover from battle wounds. He was so grateful for his recovery that he brought several doctor-priests back to Pergamum and established the Asklepieion there. Aesculapius was the god of medicine and the serpent and staff were his symbol, his icon.

The ruins of the Temple of Aesculapius are still adorned with carvings of the serpent. Serpents were also used in dark tunnels to perform certain healing rites at the Temple of Telesporos. Telesporos was considered the god of cure-revealing dreams. It also had healing fountains in the courtyard used by many known leaders of the ancient world.

In 133 B.C. the last king, Attalus III, died and bequeathed his kingdom to Rome. In the Roman era, both Marcus Aurelius and Caracalla went there to be healed.

Barack Obama's prized wedding ring which he has worn for many years, since he lived in Indonesia, long before he was married, holds two coiled serpent icons. Obviously, he treasures the serpents' relevance on his ring as did the ancients in Pergamum who worshiped their serpent icon. Furthermore, that 'old serpent' is mentioned many times in the Bible as the deceiver who tries to lead people from the words of God. According to the Bible the first encounter with that deceiving serpent was in the beginning.

Mankind's first encounter with the serpent was when he met Eve, the first woman, in the Garden of Eden. And what did the old serpent do? His first act was to deceive Eve about the fruit of the tree in the midst of the garden. This encounter is described in Genesis, Chapter 3:

"Now the serpent was more subtil than any beast of

the field which the Lord God had made. And he said
unto the woman, Yea, hath God said, Ye shall not eat
of every tree of the garden?
2 And the woman said unto the serpent, We may eat
of the fruit of the trees of the garden:
3 But of the fruit of the tree which is in th midst of the
garden, God hath said, Ye shall not eat of it, neither
shall ye touch it, lest ye die.
4 And the serpent said unto the woman, Ye shall not
surely die:
5 For God doth know that in the day ye eat thereof,
then your eyes shall be opened, and ye shall be as
gods, knowing good and evil."

The rest of that story is common history. Eve ate the fruit, supposedly
the apple, then gave some to Adam. Their eyes became open and they
were aware of right and wrong and evil and good. God sent them
from the Garden of Eden to toil the rest of their lives. And, mankind
was assigned to toil forever. The serpent was assigned to crawl on his
belly in the dust forever.

That story in Genesis was a long time ago. No one really knows how
old. During that long time the climate has changed and shifted on the
face of the earth; where rivers once flowed at the Garden of Eden,
now harsh dry land prevails; major kings and dynasties have come
and gone; and politics on the globe keep shifting always in favor of
those who control the most power.

Often that power is determined not necessarily by strength alone, but
often by deception, that same deception created by Satan in the
Garden of Eden. That old serpent is as alive today as he was in the
Garden of Eden. He takes many forms and shapes, but his actions and
words are still those of the serpent who turned mankind against the
words of God. Although the serpent is Satan's first known visible

form of deceit, it takes many forms as proclaimed by Second John 1:7:

> "For many deceivers are entered into the world, who confess not that Jesus Christ is come in the flesh. This is a deceiver and an antichrist."

Does Barack Obama follow his serpents, the seat of Satan, to also deceive American citizens? Will he deceive even more in the future?

Rules for Radicals

I got this information in an email, but forgot the origin. The sender asked recipients to 'pass it on.' It concerns the influence of Saul Alinsky on our current politics:

Saul Alinsky died about 43 years ago, but his writings continue to influence many in political control of our nation today. Hillary did her college thesis on his writings and Obama writes about him in his books.

Alinsky's important books are: 'Rules for Radicals' and 'Reveille for Radicals.' In the books he explains how to create a social state. According to him there are eight levels of control that must be obtained before you are able to create a social state. The first is the most important.

1) Healthcare– Control healthcare and you control the people.

2) Poverty – Increase the poverty level as high as possible, poor people are easier to control and will not fight back if you are providing everything for them to live.

3) Debt – Increase the debt to an unsustainable level. That way you

are able to increase taxes, and this will produce more poverty.

4) Gun Control– Remove the ability to defend themselves from the government. That way you are able to create a police state.

5) Welfare – Take control of every aspect of their lives (Food, Housing, and Income.)

6) Education – Take control of what people read and listen to – take control of what children learn in school.

7) Religion – Remove the belief in the God from the Government and schools.

8) Class Warfare – Divide the people into the wealthy and the poor. This will cause more discontent and it will be easier to take (Tax) the wealthy with the support of the poor.

Alinsky merely simplified Vladimir Lenin's original scheme for world conquest by communism, under Russian rule. Stalin described his converts as "Useful Idiots." The Useful Idiots have destroyed every nation in which they have seized power and control. It is presently happening at an alarming rate in the U.S. According to Alinsky: "It is difficult to free fools from the chains they revere."

I had never heard that term before, "Useful Idiots," so I went to Wikipedia. This is part of the Wikipedia description:

"In political jargon, useful idiot is a term for people perceived as propagandists for a cause whose goals they are not fully aware of, and who are used cynically by the leaders of the cause.

Despite often being attributed to Lenin, in 1987, Grant Harris, senior reference librarian at the Library of Congress, declared that "We have not been able to identify this phrase among [Lenin's] published works."

In Russian language, the equivalent term "useful fools" was in use at least in 1941.

A similar term, useful innocents, appears in Austrian-American economist Ludwig von Mises's "Planned Chaos" (1947). Von Mises claims the term was used by communists for liberals that von Mises describes as "confused and misguided sympathizers". The term useful innocents also appears in a Readers Digest article (1946) titled "Yugoslavia's Tragic Lesson to the World", an excerpt from a, at the time, forthcoming book (no title printed) authored by Bogdan Raditsa (Bogdan Radica), a "high ranking official of the Yugoslav Government". Raditsa says: "In the Serbo-Croat language the communists have a phrase for true democrats who consent to collaborate with them for 'democracy.' It is Korisne Budale, or Useful Innocents." Although Raditsa translates the phrase as "Useful Innocents", the word budala (plural: budale) actually translates as "fool" and synonyms thereof."

Interesting. Do any of the eight rules and the terms listed above seem connected to current events here in America? How many does Barack Obama routinely address, and advocate, in his speeches, proposals, and with his pen? All!

Edward Snowden

Edward Snowden: patriot or traitor? Many of us have asked this same question. Our opinions about this man are certainly varied and are guided by our backgrounds, our experiences, our prejudices and our political leanings. So far, I can't get a firm fix on my opinion of this man. My vacillation, however, is not based on Snowden's actions or intentions. My opinion is based on my trust or distrust about the intentions of our government, specifically Barack Obama.

My big dilemma of trust or distrust is: which one of these men poses the greatest danger to America? Edward Snowden is just one man who can be classified as a traitor. Do his actions so far suggest he's a man determined to harm America, or simply trying to alert citizens to the serious dangers posed by our government? On the other hand, Barack Obama has the power and platform to preserve a great nation - or destroy it. How can a man who tells so many lies and falsehoods be trusted to fulfill his sworn duty? Do actions and comments always reveal intentions?

Could one imagine Snowden plans great harm to America? Could one imagine Barack Obama plans great harm to our freedoms and democracy? What are some clues?

So far, as far as we know, Snowden has released only information that alerts us to the depths of government spying against American citizens, especially that data gathered at the new NSA spy center in Bluffdale, Utah. If left unchecked, how far would the government go to delve into every corner of every citizens' lives - in the name of fighting terrorism? Unchecked, likely there would be no stopping them until all our freedoms have been suppressed.

And, what do we know about the Obama administration? Lies, deceptions, falsehoods, coverups, denials, and more restrictions every day that limit our freedoms. They are Obama's 'pen' and new daily regulations that bypass our leaders in Congress, duly elected to protect our freedom. Why are they bypassing that check and balance system designed to protect us?

So, who presents the most danger to our great nation? Is Edward Snowden the traitor?

My latest book: 'Death Drones 2025,' gives a description of the danger of allowing a government to delve too deeply into every person's private lives - especially their everyday purchases, which the NSA will have the capability to do when we convert to a cashless society. Coming soon? When we convert to a cashless society - and we will soon - the government will know - instantly - everything about us, and all our connections. How will they use that knowledge? That's the question.

How Close are the Terrorists?

Recently, I returned from another driving trip, from Mississippi to California, to visit our children and grandchildren. I retired from the Air Force there in 1978, so that's still their home. Their numbers have blossomed from: children, grandchildren, and now 3 great-grandchildren. Years ago my job moved me back to Mississippi, where my wife and I remained. We are originally from this area and still have relatives nearby. Since we are now the eldest in our two families, we decided to remain here in case the others needed help.

During the driving trip to California and back two things reminded me of my writings and the events happening in our great nation. In my book: 'America 20XX,' I fictionally wrote that Islamic terrorists were infiltrating into the U.S. through the desert south of Casa Grande, Arizona, to become pre-positioned moles waiting for a certain event to occur before they became active infiltrators. Two weeks after I published that book, Border Patrol agents found an Islamic book titled, 'In Memory of our Martyrs' in that same desert in that same location I had described. During that trip I stayed one night at a hotel in Casa Grande and had time to look south and wonder if that idea could really become real. Why was that book found in that location? This is the link describing that book:

http://factsnotfairies.blogspot.com/2011/01/in-memory-of-our-mart

yrs-in-az-desert.html

I also had another surprise, something new, that reminded me of my latest novel, 'Death Drones 2025.' Each of the eight times I registered at a hotel I was asked for my driver's license. At first I thought it was only to match the name with the name on my credit card to insure it wasn't a stolen credit card. I was surprised when the clerk entered my license number into the computer. This wasn't random - it was all eight times. I wondered once my identity was confirmed - why did they need to enter my license number? Then it struck me up side the head like a bazooka: the NSA and Bluffdale, Utah. I have no doubt this information went straight into the limitless information storage center there. My first inclination was to say, "Who cares?" But then reality and ideas from my book slapped me right in the face. Everything the government does is important - and it leads to further encroachment on our freedoms. I asked, "Could the next step be that described in my book for total government control of every citizen?"

That next step before total government control (totalitarianism) is a cashless society. Since everything and everybody will be controlled by numbers and computers - why is cash necessary? Remember the information in Revelation, Chapter 13, Verses 17 and 18. One must have the 'mark of the beast' to buy and sell. In my opinion, that means cash will no longer be used. Likely, one who tried to barter or use cash or cash equivalents will be branded as a terrorist and killed - beheaded.

Keep watching. When the government says we no longer need cash it will sound like a wonderful and rational idea, and will be readily accepted by many. And it might be. But the bigger question becomes: what happens next? This link takes you to the NSA Bluffdale Center.

http://en.wikipedia.org/wiki/Utah_Data_Center

Who is the 666 beast - the Antichrist?

When I wrote the book, '666: Mark of the Beast,' I read just enough passages in the Bible's Book of Revelation to have a general guide for the major plot of the book. It's been a while since I completed that project, and although I'm enjoying the rest break, I'm thinking about writing a new novel based on the entirety of the Book of Revelation. To do that of course, I need more understanding. I have been reading Revelation every day for several months trying for more interpretation. One night, recently, something jumped off the page and slapped me between the eyes.

In Chapter 13: Verse 18, John wrote: "Here is wisdom. Let him that hath understanding count the number of the beast: for it is the number of a man; and his number is Six hundred threescore and six." (666) Professionals have long tried to interpret those numbers through association with the Greek alphabet. Would someone trying to tell us something that important create a cryptic puzzle too complicated to understand? Let's simplify John's information.

"count the number of the beast for it is the number of a man;" John said count; he didn't say interpret. If we count 6+6+6, we get 18. Now, let's say the beast's name will have 18 letters. That's counting; it's what John said to do. Now, use your imagination to picture a possible candidate of our times who has 18 letters in his full name. Surprised? one name fits perfectly.

BARACKHUSSEINOBAMA

Now for the ironic part; John must have had a sense of humor, even at the age of a hundred. His 6+6+6 is **18**. Was it a joke, or irony, that John put this information in Verse **18**?

Is a nation accepting ungodly acts also defiled?

http://biblehub.com/revelation/13-1.htm

"Leviticus 18 lists many acts of nakedness and sexual activity such as adultery and incest not tolerated by God. Verses 22 and 23 specifically identify homosexuality as an abomination, and bestiality as confusion. However as Leviticus pertains to America, and other countries, verses 24 through 28 are most applicable.

In summary, those verses state that if a nation accepts these ungodly actions by its individuals then that nation is also defiled: "therefore I do visit the iniquity thereof upon it, and the land itself vomiteth out her inhabitants." 27: "For all these abominations have the men of the land done, which were before you, and the land it defiled." 28: That the land spue not you out also, when ye defile it, as it spued out the nations that were before you."

Perhaps this next article gives an example. It's from Godfatherpolitics.com. It was submitted by Dave Jolly in September, 2013. The article begins:

"Gay activists are successfully getting laws passed in cities around the country that discriminate against Christians. The laws are called nondiscrimination laws by the LGBT activists pushing through one city council after another. So far, over 180 cities have passed these so-called nondiscrimination ordinances.

In essence the laws provide special protection to LGBT individuals while at the same time; they place huge restrictions on the religious rights of Christians. For instance, the San Antonio city council voted 8-3 to pass their ordinance that bans any form of discrimination based upon sexual orientation or gender identity. Their ban went so far as to forbid anyone who does not openly accept or support gay rights from conducting any business with the city. Violating the ordinance is a Class C misdemeanor that could result in a fine of up to $500 per day.

If a pastor is preaching on Sunday and says anything about homosexuality being a sin in the eyes of God, he could be arrested for violating the ordinance. If you are in a private conversation with someone and say that you believe homosexuality is a sin or that you are uncomfortable around someone because they are gay, you could be arrested. The way LGBT activists operate these days, I can see them visiting churches just to try to catch the pastor or someone else saying anything against homosexuality just so they can run to the city to have them arrested.

This is the concern of many Christian leaders throughout San Antonio and other cities that have passed similar laws. Jacob Herrera with Faith Outreach International commented, saying:

"The right for us to speak out and say, 'I disagree. It doesn't sound right.' Now we're labeled a hater, a bigot, homophobic."

Rosalie Astran, a member of Abundant Life Church reacted to San Antonio's ordinance saying:

"My faith, my belief and how I've raised my family—I can get in trouble for that because they don't agree with that."

Carleton Soules, San Antonio Councilman who voted no on the ordinance was deeply concerned about how the ordinance was rushed thru the system. He stated:

"We didn't put the ordinance up on the website. It was fast-tracked through. Anytime we are going at light speed to do something that's unpopular that throws a lot of red flags."

"I believe if you're a small business owner, operating within the city limits of San Antonio, or you're a business owner that wants to do business with the city, you need to tread carefully."

These non (or anti) discrimination ordinances echo the hate language measures that the United Nations has been trying to push on everyone. One thing they all have in common is that it is illegal to discriminate against anyone for race, gender, gender identification, sexual orientation and religion, provided you're not a Christian. It's perfectly legal and allowable to discriminate against Christians and restrict their rights of religion and free speech. We seem to be the only demographic group that can be slandered, insulted, urinated on, and told what we are and are not allowed to say. In some areas like California, homosexuals can counsel and provide therapy for those confused about their sexual orientation, but Christians are not legally allowed to provide the same counseling and therapy to the same confused individuals.

Today, we find nearly 200 cities with nondiscriminatory ordinances. By the end of the year the number will most likely be well over 200. It wouldn't surprise me to see a federal law passed sometime before the end of 2014 that discriminates against Christians and provides the special protection for gays. If left unchecked, by the end of 2015 we could well see any public show of Christianity to be outlawed because it offends someone somewhere. No one cares about offending Christians because we're just lower class citizens anyway." End of Article.

What are Their Plans?

Inequality, fair share, higher pay, more rights, more free stuff, more encouragement of anti-Bible and ungodly activity; these are the things Barack Obama has focused on to maintain his power. These are the same fundamentals Hillary Clinton will focus on during her upcoming quest, the unending quest, to become president of the

United States. These were the foundation bricks of Barack Obama's successful drive to become president. Certainly, Hillary will not stray far from that same tactic if she decides to campaign for president.

It's the tactic described in George Orwell's book, '1984.' To summarize this approach: the lows are used by the middle to advance themselves to the highs. The lows think they will be advanced to the middle - but that never happens. After their users, the middle, are successful, the lows are returned back to the low status until they are used again in that same cycle. The lows NEVER advance. They are only useful tools for the more ambitious. The lows are so insignificant and predictable they are not even monitored by Orwell's Big Brother.

Her target audience will be those without ambition or aspirations, poor people, the growing uneducated population, and certain other special interest groups outside the guidance of Judeo-Christian beliefs. These are the people without a firm foundation that permits them to have self-grounded beliefs and aspirations offered by the blessing of God. How can a solid structure be built without first having a steady foundation? Most of those considered the low by Orwell don't even understand those foundational concepts so they can strive toward them.

Using the Obama model she will prey upon the weak, lazy, uneducated, and those who don't understand the underlying concepts that define socialism and capitalism - and the resulting differences of each. Too many don't understand or accept the idea that under socialism a few government leaders define success and prosperity for citizens. Under capitalism, the citizens define the purpose for government and have freedom to define success for themselves.

Those with the grounded aspirations of confidence and belief realize they must work hard to be successful - and must never stray from the guiding beacon ahead. Education, a positive attitude, and hard work are the ladders to success. Success doesn't happen by accident - it's not a choice off a silver platter. Neither are security, safety, and a life of comfort as promised by Barack Obama - and soon Hillary Clinton - to get votes to fulfill their personal ambitions of power and influence. Instead, shouldn't they guide themselves with honesty so American citizens can make the right choice about who is honorable enough to lead our great nation?

Once Barack Obama reached his high level, the lows - those who put him there - were lowered back into their lower positions just as Orwell described. Poverty and food stamps have increased since he was elected president. But he still promises. His promises are to keep that higher door open for Hillary Clinton. Her goal is to reach that high place any way she can - even off the backs and dreams of the low who will be enchanted to support her. She has a great smile and great words designed to deceive those lows who pledge total allegiance to her.

Will the lows be better off if and when Hillary Clinton were to be elected president? History reveals they will be disappointed and disregarded - but they will still dream of their savior doing great things for them. Shades of George Orwell and '1984.'

The other more dire option must also be considered. Obama has demonstrated time and again that he does not respect the United States Constitution and our country's laws. Will he step aside at the end of his term to allow Hillary to campaign? Trends, and his actions, suggest he will not.

Will truth, honesty, integrity, and the words of God be disregarded for the evil struggle for more power? Will God and His teachings be denied again by the group that denied His name three times on the Democratic National Convention stage seen world-wide in 2012? All signs are that the answer is yes. Not only is His name being denied, it's also being cast out and blasphemed on more stages every day world-wide and in the United States. Barack Obama is leading the attack on God and Christianity. Most likely, the first target to suffer from his influences, actions, and inactions is Israel, particularly the city of Jerusalem.

Insert

Daniel 7:23 refers to the 'fourth' beast which is also considered as the last antichrist. But, the really important part of this reference is that the fourth kingdom 'will be diverse from all kingdoms, and shall devour the whole earth.' Prior to this, all the kingdoms have included only bits and pieces of the earth, usually contained only within continents. Again, this reference says, "shall devour the whole earth, and shall tread it down, and break it to pieces." Certainly, the whole world would be a kingdom diverse from all other kingdoms.

Combining these references, it's a logical conclusion to suggest only one thing. There will come an antichrist, or beast; and he will arise when the seven continents, the whole earth, is controlled by one kingdom - the one diverse from all others. Revelation 12:9 also says Satan will deceive the 'whole world' when he was cast out of Heaven. But, what will the beast look like? How will we recognize him? To do that, let's consider the other part of Chapter 13:2:

> "And the beast which I saw was like unto a leopard,
> and his feet were as the feet of a bear, and his mouth
> as the mouth of a lion–"

Here one must consider the obvious traits or characteristics of each animal. A leopard is a cat; which would suggest stealth, guile and deception. A bear is known for its strength; and perhaps as a strength to influence others. A lion is known for its great roar, the attention he gets from his mouth. Perhaps to identify the beast destined to destroy our lives, we must consider a person who exemplifies these three major characteristics.

End of Insert

Conclusion

Islamists plan to destroy Western civilization. It's their final destiny; it's all they dream of and plan. It's in their thoughts, their writings, and their strategies. They are not subtle about that mission. They throw it in our faces and dare us to resist. They want us to resist for an excuse to kill - behead - more human beings.

They must first remove the 'one that restrains' to proceed with that mission. Some people believe this relates to the time of the 'Rapture' when all believers will suddenly and miraculously be taken to Heaven - and will just disappear from the face of the earth and rule with Christ for the Millennium, that thousand years. This is not the case at all.

First, the word or the idea of a Rapture, as interpreted, does not exist in the Bible. Second, only the souls of those beheaded for not denying their Christian faith, and refusing the mark of the beast during this period, will occupy that Millennial position as explained in Revelation 20:4-6. This is identified as the 'first resurrection.' The 'second resurrection' includes all others as explained in 20:12-13. This is where the other souls are judged from the 'book of life - according to their works.'

119

http://www.bibleexplained.com/revelation/r-seg19-20/r20b-
v4.htm

Many Americans are now training with the Sunni takeover in Iraq.
Will they later begin terrorist attacks in America to create a
condition of fear that will allow Obama to claim a national
emergency and martial law, and refuse to step down as president at
the time stipulated in our Constitution? Perhaps the Iranian threat
of a nuclear attack, and their Mahdi, will be other factors supporting
Obama's claim of a national emergency. If this happens will this be
the end of humanity and freedom as we understand it in human and
religious terms?

What might be the first significant signs to warn of that coming
event? First, more confusion and terrorist attacks will occur on our
southern borders. Second, many Christians will be targeted as
terrorists - or as supporters of terrorism. Finally, cash transactions
will be eliminated under the guise of fighting terrorism. When that
happens, everyone must make the choice to accept or not accept the
mark of the beast so they can buy and sell. It will be a final and
deadly choice for Christians.

**Will our government use deadly force against American
citizens?**

Will government forces fire on their fellow citizens - these
Christians who will be proclaimed 'terrorists' by our government?
Yes - absolutely; and there are past examples. Consider only two;
David Koresh and Randy Weaver.

This note from Wikipedia briefly describes that David Koresh
(Branch Davidians) incident:

"David Koresh (born Vernon Wayne Howell; August 17, 1959 –

120

April 19, 1993) was the American leader of the Branch Davidians religious sect, believing himself to be its final prophet. Howell legally changed his name to David Koresh on May 15, 1990 (Koresh being the Persian name of Cyrus the Great; Kurosh). A 1993 raid by the U.S. Bureau of Alcohol, Tobacco, Firearms and Explosives, and the subsequent siege by the FBI ended with the burning of the Branch Davidian ranch outside of Waco, Texas, in McLennan County. Koresh, 54 other adults, and 28 children were found dead after the fire." Neither Koresh nor any of his followers had been clearly charged with a crime.

History.com gives a summary of the Randy Weaver - Ruby Ridge incident:

"In the second day of a standoff at Randy Weaver's remote northern Idaho cabin, FBI sharpshooter Lon Horiuchi wounds Randy Weaver, Kevin Harrison, and kills Weaver's wife, Vicki.

Randy Weaver, a white separatist, had been targeted by the federal government after failing to appear in court to face charges related to his selling of two illegal sawed-off shotguns to an Alcohol, Tobacco and Firearms (ATF) informant. On August 21, 1992, after a period of surveillance, U.S. marshals came upon Harrison; Weaver; Weaver's 14-year-old son, Sammy; and the family dog, Striker, on a road near the Weaver property. A marshal shot and killed the dog, prompting Sammy to fire at the marshal. In the ensuing gun battle, Sammy and U.S. Marshal Michael Degan were shot and killed. A tense standoff ensued, and on August 22 the FBI joined the marshals besieging Ruby Ridge.

Later that day, Harris, Weaver, and his daughter, Sarah, left the cabin, allegedly for the purpose of preparing Sammy's body for burial. FBI sharpshooter Lon Horiuchi, waiting 200 yards away, opened fire, allegedly because he thought Harrison was armed and intending to fire on a helicopter in the vicinity. Horiuchi wounded Weaver, and the group ran to the shed where Sammy's body was lying. When they attempted to escape back into the cabin, Horiuchi fired again, wounding Harrison as he dove through the door and killing Vicki Weaver, who was holding the door open with one hand and cradling her infant daughter with the other. Horiuchi claimed he didn't know that Vicki Weaver was standing behind the door. Harris, Weaver, and Weaver's three daughters surrendered nine days later.

In 1993, Weaver and Harris were acquitted by a federal court on murder, conspiracy, and other charges related to Degan's death, but Weaver was convicted of failing to appear for trial on the firearms charge. In 1994, the two men filed federal civil rights cases against the FBI and U.S. marshals stemming from the siege, and in 1995 the government settled Weaver's case for $3.1 million."

The incident was instigated by the agents. They didn't know the trial date had been changed to a later date. Innocent people were killed by the government."

Would our government agents, or our military, hesitate to fire on terrorists if ordered to do so by our government leaders? How soon and under what conditions will many Christians be proclaimed 'terrorists' by a tyrannical government? How could our government troops refuse to fire? Perhaps this was the meaning of the warning in Revelation for believers to 'flee to the wilderness.'

On two occasions God has been denied three times; first by his closest follower, Peter; then on a world stage at the 2012 Democratic National Convention. There's a philosophical saying about the 'third time.' Is that third time fast approaching? Should we be concerned?

God bless America.

About the Author

Will Clark's author experiences began by writing inspection and evaluation reports in the U.S. Air Force. He is a retired Air Force officer and a Vietnam veteran, serving in Saigon from 1966 to 1967. His other overseas assignments include Misawa, Japan and Ankara, Turkey.

In 1995, he authored a book, *How to Learn*, as a county-wide study skills project to encourage students to improve their grades in DeSoto County, Mississippi. Education supporters printed and distributed four thousand copies. He also wrote a weekly education column for a local newspaper, *The Desoto County Tribune,* the following school year.

His next published book was *School Bells and Broken Tales*, a parody of nursery rhyme characters, also a motivation and education book for children. His other books include *Shades of Retribution*, a historical novel, and *Simply Success*, a motivation guide for students and employees.

His action novels include a trilogy based on Atlantis and crystals. The first book is titled: *The Atlantis Crystal.* The second book is titled: *She Waits In Atlantis.* The third is: *Return to Atlantis.* This trilogy is based on his travels while assigned to Turkey, site of the ancient city of Troy.

His previous political action novel, *666: Mark of the Beast*, is a sequel to another political action novel, *America 20XX: The New World Order.*

Clark and his wife, Marie, live in Diamondhead, Mississippi, where they play golf with many friends.

For more information about the author visit:

http://www.authorsden.com/visit/author.asp?authorid=1496

Things We Must Never Forget
Until We Know All the Answers

Benghazi

Why were four Americans killed?
Where was Hillary Clinton while it was happening?
Where was Barack Obama while it was happening?
Why did they lie and blame the event on a video?
Why were rescuers on 'stand by' told to 'stand down?'

Fast and Furious

Who authorized the operation?
Why did the operation continue after weapons were lost?
Why did the procedure have no procedure?
Why weren't tracking devices used?

The IRS Scandal

What was the highest level involved?
Who initiated it?
Why hasn't anyone been fired or reprimanded?
What dangers could be unleashed by this organization?

Greatest Quotes
of
Our Time

Michelle Obama
February 18, 2008
"For the first time in my adult life I am proud of my country."
(Age 44)

Barack Obama
March 9, 2008
"We are no longer a Christian nation - at least not just."

Nancy Pelosi
March 9, 2010
"We have to pass the bill so that you can find out what is in it."

Hillary Clinton
January 23, 2013
"What difference, at this point, does it make?"

Other Books by the Author

Novels:
Shades of Retribution
The Atlantis Crystal
She Waits in Atlantis
Return to Atlantis
America 20XX: The New World Order
666: Mark of the Beast
Death Drones: 2025

Children's Books:
Forest Trails and Fairy Tales
Wishing Wells and Broken Tales
Student Study Skills
American Heroes: Students Who Learn

Non-Fiction:
Simply Success
The Education Jungle
How to Learn
The Day America Died
Obama's Ring: The Seat of Satan
Managing Without Conflict
The Peer Pressure Monster